THE ROYAL FAMILY

THE
ROYAL FAMILY
At Home and Abroad

TREVOR HALL

Colour Library Books

All photographs © **REX FEATURES LIMITED**

Featuring the photography of **David Levenson**
and Nils Jorgensen, Peter Brooker, Dave Hartley, Mauro Carraro, "Today",
Brendan Bierne and Richard Young

Text and captions by Trevor Hall

Production Director
Gerald Hughes

Editorial Director
David Gibbon

CLB 2211
Copyright © 1989 Colour Library Books Ltd.,
Godalming, Surrey.
Colour separations by Hong Kong Graphic Arts Ltd., Hong Kong.
Printed and bound in Italy.

ISBN 0 86283 652 2

'Being royal,' said Princess Margaret's son recently, 'is not such a big deal in London these days'. Almost as he spoke these words, the strongly republican-orientated government of Australia was putting the finishing touches to plans to welcome no fewer than eight members of the Royal Family to its shores for the biggest birthday party Australia has ever had – the Bicentennial celebrations.

The contrast in these two attitudes says a lot about both the Royal Family and ourselves. 'The British, bless them,' said a politician once, 'do hate emotion'. For that reason as much as any, they tend to take their Royal Family, which satisfies an emotional rather than a political need, for granted. Dwellers beyond the United Kingdom, on the contrary, do not seem able to get enough of royalty, especially if it's British. Whether this is because they have left their British homeland and yearn nostalgically for its traditions, as in Canada, South Africa, Australia and New Zealand; or whether they once had their own monarchy and have since disposed of it, as in West Germany, Italy, Mexico and China; or whether they never had a crowned head and perhaps wish they had, like the United States, is always open to speculation. But certain it is that any member of the Royal Family travelling abroad is assured of a public reception that would put most Britons to shame.

Some have defined monarchy in the British style as glorified soap opera; others as the expression of all that is best in tradition and the embodiment of a benign development of political maturity. Some find it grossly over-expensive; others regard its cost as a small price to pay for a splash of colour in a drab and anxious world. Some argue that its influence and enormous financial privileges emphasise the nation's social divisions; others are equally convinced that in some unexplained way it unites the nation and provides a focus for stability. Many think we can do without it. Many fear the enormous hole that would be left by its disappearance.

None of these considerations is without sincere foundation; each can be tenably argued, yet only in conjunction with the others. In other words, this is no black-and-white phenomenon; there are many grey areas. And the reason for these grey areas is primarily that the monarchy in Britain has been modifying itself over the centuries – and particularly during the last few decades – to the formula required of it by its public. The Queen knows, as everybody should, that, despite the Crown's symbols of power, the monarchy is in place only by the will of Parliament, and that Parliament exists according to the will of the people. If popular support for the monarchy wanes, and more especially if it mutates into active hostility, then through or despite Parliament, the Crown will vanish. This is why for so long, the watchword for successive sovereigns has been 'adapt'.

The process of adaptation has been continuous, if at times slow. Queen Victoria's reign saw the effects of social conscience on the Crown, which is why so many members of her family became associated with charities. Today, there is hardly an official royal engagement that is not linked with a charity or well-deserving cause, and the idea seems somehow to have proliferated since the Princess of Wales came onto the scene. Her natural empathy with children was well known from the start, and accounts for the huge number of children's organisations with which she is connected, as well as for the pronounced informality that, to the delight of all onlookers, has characterised her meetings with them. From this has sprung an equally obvious concern for those suffering the worst misfortunes of poverty, illness and old age, and a brave foray into the darker realms of drug abuse and AIDS. Not long ago, these would have been subjects on which royalty, like the rest of us, would have preferred to turn its back. But when Diana appeared on television to give her support to a no-holds-barred anti-drugs campaign, and later visited a hospice for HIV sufferers and shook hands, for all to see, with an AIDS victim, public attention found new focuses and many myths and misunderstandings were nailed.

5

Although there is no match for Diana, and the winning way in which she fulfils her public role, one suspects that much of the impetus has come from Prince Charles. With an independent income from the Duchy of Cornwall, there is every encouragement for him to lead a life of leisure. Yet he is so socially aware, and so conscious of his need to adapt, that much of his energy is being channelled to such causes as community schemes in Wales, the disadvantaged young in inner cities, nature conservation and architecture. Most of his activities in these areas have come in for praise, except for what many see as his criticism of Government attitudes towards urban decay, and what others see as a reactionary interference in new architectural plans. It doesn't bother Prince Charles. On the first point, he replies that if they don't like what he says here, he will go somewhere else and say it. On the second, he claims that he is much closer to the wishes of the people who have to live in, visit, or merely look at new architectural schemes than the boffins who dream them up in some faceless office.

Charles and Diana make a superb team when they go abroad. They see comparatively little of each other on official engagements at home, and a foreign trip often gives them the opportunity to spark off each other – and frequently in public. In the early part of their marriage, this took the form of a few lines of fulsome praise by Charles towards his wife, and an embarrassed grimace from Diana in return. Now, more confident, Diana sees the funny side of some royal duties, and the comparatively informal atmosphere abroad gives her the opportunity to express it. On over-organised walkabouts she has more than once confused officials by dragging Charles over from his side of the street to speak to somebody on her side, and has herself occasionally nipped across the lines to respond to persistent pleas from the crowd. And when, in Australia, the couple had to wear protective hats during a factory tour, Diana was helpless with laughter when she saw Charles' badly-fitting helmet perched on his head like a shiny gold bubble. Charles, perhaps a little exasperated, said to the nearest man: 'Does your wife make fun of you like this?' It didn't stop Diana's giggles.

Brother Andrew and sister-in-law Sarah are another royal couple who are proving – in the words of Prince Philip – well adjusted to each other. In their first two years they have made several trips abroad, of which the tour of Canada and the visit to California were memorable for their spectacle and colour. The Canadian journey lacked a serious purpose in the routine royal sense, and became something of a sightseeing holiday interspersed with banquets and the occasional duty visit. It was criticised by some as a fortnight of light comedy, a description that owes much to Sarah's spontaneous sense of fun, to which she gave full rein: she punched her husband on the shoulder when a piece of wadding from a starting pistol he was using flew in her face, and she throttled him in mock revenge at a banquet after he slipped in a reference to her hair as 'wild and woolly'. In California, she interrupted one of Andrew's speeches to remind him to say 'we' and not 'I', and while he was sampling some of the more gentle thrills of a simulated high-speed road-roller, she called out to their hosts to 'take him for a *real* spin!' which they did – much, no doubt, to the detriment of the royal insides.

The advent of the Duchess of York, with her unabashed, outgoing personality, has not been universally welcomed. Some have found her appearance and behaviour overdone, flashy, essentially un-royal. A well-publicised news item showing her and Princess Diana at Royal Ascot, both young ladies giggling and stabbing other members of the royal party in the legs with their umbrellas, confirmed for many the feeling that Sarah's bubbly personality was developing into something of a bad influence. Others felt that the participation of Prince Andrew, the Princess Royal and Prince Edward in the television spectacular *It's A Royal Knockout* owed too much to her frivolity, and that her ebulliently sporty contribution to it was no more than empty clowning. Opinions on the subject have differed ever since, and if Sarah feels she has gone too far, she will, all in good time, adjust . Again, it's all part of the royal syndrome of adapting to public need or expectation.

Princess Anne discovered for herself what it means to adapt, and in particular that the Press can be pretty fickle when it comes to reporting on royalty. On her royal debut, she was hailed as a royal fashion heroine – the Swinging Princess, a cliché she rejected then on the grounds that she felt she was 'really rather staid.' Then, as she concentrated on her equestrian career, her attempts to discourage the Press spoiling her performance by taking pictures of her during competitions were reported as rudeness and arrogance, while vivid descriptions of her colourful language prompted one five-year-old to ask: 'Who learnt Princess Anne to swear?' By the beginning of the 1980s, the knives were being withdrawn again as the media realised that there was rather more to the Princess than a snorting bad temper and a graphic vocabulary. Her tours of underdeveloped countries in search of ways in which relief agencies could help prevent or deal with the appalling consequences of famine, disease and ignorance became more frequent, and her questing, thrusting attitudes in addressing the problem – not to say her willingness to live and work in conditions which were basic at best, uncomfortable on average, and filthy at worst – won her widespread, enduring and, even the least sympathetic observer would agree, justifiable praise. She often said she wanted a real career, and even showed a penchant for lorry-driving once; perhaps she now feels that, if her work for the Save the Children Fund allows her a little time to train as a steeplechase jockey, she has unearthed a career of immensely satisfying properties.

Perhaps this is also true of Prince Edward, though as it is comparatively soon, in career terms, since he quit the Royal Marines, perhaps it's too early to say. His is a classic case of deciding how far a life in the royal mould is desirable, or even necessary. Like his sister, he has in his time been vilified by the Press as being pompous, jumped-up, too clever by half, and his public and private altercations with them reflected little credit on either, save that he had the courage, despite his tender years, to tackle adversaries of some experience. He may well feel that his love of the theatre and his organising ability, both so fully evidenced during his three years at Cambridge, are skills best put to use now, and he has found the appropriate outlet with a London theatre company. In the meantime, he is carrying out a token round of royal duties on a minimum allowance, and may well continue to do so until he decides how he can best balance his preference for a meaningful career where he can lead, and the demands upon him merely to follow the routine, however privileged, of royalty.

No such agonisings trouble his cousins. The children of Princess Margaret, the Gloucesters, Kents and Ogilvys are, or will be, able and entitled to pursue their chosen careers in the knowledge that duties of a royal nature will almost certainly never be required of them. Thus Viscount Linley has already shaped his future in furniture-making, while his sister, Lady Sarah Armstrong-Jones, is making first strides in the art and design world. Of the Duke of Kent's children, the Earl of St Andrews has just completed his post-graduate degree in social anthropology at Cambridge, where his wife is a research Fellow in history; Lady Helen Windsor has been following a career in the business of the Arts, while Lord Nicholas, having rounded off his A-level course at Harrow, has joined an Operation Raleigh expedition in East Africa. In this he has emulated his cousin, Princess Alexandra's daughter Marina, whose own career may well be a musical one, while her newly-married brother James has completed his Arts degree at St Andrew's University.

For the Gloucester children, and those of Prince Michael, too, careers of their choosing lie ahead. How different for the Wales children and the York baby. These, and any further brothers and sisters, will be brought up to come to terms with the fact that they are royal, and to recognise and respect the consequent obligations in preparation for life in an unremitting royal mould. In this, however, they have one big advantage over the Prince of Wales, who was heir to the Throne from the age of three: they will almost certainly be able at least to live out their childhood and adolescence while their parents are unencumbered with the serious and daily duties of sovereignty, and thus avoid some of the searching spotlight that focused on Charles from his very earliest days, and gave him what he later called that 'ghastly, inexorable sense' of being the object of unnerving public attention.

If the monarchy is adapting in all these areas, it is because such changes have the encouragement of the Queen herself. This may seem strange, because the Queen is an essentially conservative person with a strong sense of her ancestry, her country's history and the traditions of the society over which she reigns. She does not nurture the convictions that give the impetus for change, but she has come to recognise that change must occur, and that her two allies in bringing it about are her two closest confidantes. When it comes to the style in which the public sees her, she has the Queen Mother to thank for showing how easy charm and unaffected human reactions can make even the most uninteresting public duties memorable for those involved. You have only to compare the majestic, but aloof and rather stilted demeanour of the late Queen Mary, whose lack of spontaneity made – as Lord Reith put it – 'rather hard going' of any host's endeavours, with the fluid, graceful enjoyment with which our Queen Mother carries out her (unfortunately, all too few) duties, to appreciate how important this influence is. Elizabeth II is said to have taken her lead from Queen Mary in many respects, but must also concede that the present Queen Mother certainly knows how to perform!

But the content and presentation of the monarchy's role has also changed since the Queen's accession, though it might not have done so but for the imaginative efforts of Prince Philip. He it is who has engineered at least some of the snobbery out of royal connections, by persuading the Queen to abolish debutante receptions at the Palace and replace them with garden parties and luncheons for an infinitely wider range of guests, varying from City magnates to snooker players and from television celebrities to postmen; by involving himself – and doubtless encouraging his children to involve themselves – in an unprecedented wealth of public causes both national and international; by making a going concern out of many royal enterprises, particularly in farming; and above all by convincing the Queen to make full use of the media. In this last area he, and therefore the Queen and Royal Family as a whole, have been supremely successful. With the television film *Royal Family*, screened to coincide with Prince Charles' Investiture in 1969, the monarchy finally came to terms with the need to admit its human face, while the showing of the television series *Royal Heritage* at the time of the Queen's Silver Jubilee eight years later projected an apt blend of that humanity and the cult and historical splendour of the Crown as a repository of ceremonial wealth and the artistic culture which has traditionally embodied it.

So, to the extent that we now accept that the Royal Family is a collection of mere human beings (which, obvious as it may be to us today, was not always thought to be the case), Viscount Linley may well be right in implying that being royal does not have the pull it once did, while the fact that its continuing history means that the family story is being constantly unfurled in public lends credence to those who regard its existence as a soap opera. On the other hand, and by the same token, a longer-term and more mature view must accept that many royal happenings are, like many human events, of an ephemeral nature, often blown up to a degree of importance unjustified by the lapse of time and the resumption of reason, while the royal institution merely adapts to meet the demands of the next decade or century. The Abdication, Prince Philip's outspokenness, the cost of *Britannia*, Princess Margaret's private life, lapses in royal security, the state of royal marriages – all have caused controversy, major or minor, and speculation. But provided the monarchy, and those into whose hands it falls, know how to maintain popular support and understanding, both at home and abroad, it will continue to withstand the effects of what at the time may seem insuperable problems. The Crown's survival, Prince Charles once said, can be measured only in direct ratio to the respect people have for it. And, as he's going to be the next king, the remark could not have come from a more appropriate quarter.

Royalty, once synonymous with monarchy, is now pretty well all that is left of it. The Queen has little real power in Britain, save the residual prerogatives which only a political vacuum would bestow. She has, however, substantial and indefinable influence, enormous financial and social privileges, an ancestry closely interlocked with the history of her country, and the unmatchable breeding to go with it. Add to this a presidential position over a country which, in spite of its egalitarian pretensions, still largely favours the trappings of outmoded monarchy and closely follows the personal and strictly private lives of the sovereign's family, and you have today's concept of royalty in Britain. The image of royalty counts for everything in a society which is profoundly image-conscious. Images can, of course, become bland stereotypes, meaningless or misleading clichés. Yet, with great care and stage-management, the British Royal Family has nursed, shaped and projected its popular image every bit as much as the media have by turns hyped and trivialised it according to the mood of the hour. Presenting any one image of royalty is therefore skating on thin ice: circumstance and the vagaries of public opinion are liable to kick the image-maker in the teeth. Having said which, here are two pictures which state at least one version of the image of British royalty today. Above, a sixty-year-old Queen with almost 35 years of presidential experience behind her; a somewhat matriarchal figure, yet surrounded by hundreds of children who thronged a palace forecourt on that very birthday to proffer thousands of daffodils; a reserved, unchanging personality whose only concessions to her young public are the vivid yellow outfit, the beaming smile and the will to walk among them. And opposite, the young woman who weathered public speculation on the state of her marriage to accomplish a stunning official visit to Germany: delightfully informal, sympathique (as the French would have it) and youthful, yet possessing now a maturity and a degree of loveliness which seemed a far cry when she walked down the aisle on Prince Charles' arm on that memorable day in 1981. Age and youth, formality and spontaneity, experience and experiment: these are the blends that perpetuate the concept and project the image of royalty today. The following pictures in this book are there to fill in the detail.

The Queen's eldest son chose his wife well. That brought the choice of bride for Prince Andrew, her second son, under intense public scrutiny, with many comparisons between the former Lady Diana and Sarah Ferguson in the months before – and indeed since – the York marriage. In doing so, many people seem to have forgotten that Diana was herself regarded as innovative and fuss-free back in 1981. Things have necessarily changed since, and her approach to her public work has been modified, if fairly imperceptibly. When Sarah came on the scene, her bubbly, spontaneous, fun-loving nature was often misinterpreted: facial contortions were seen as over-the-top; gesticulations as a touch common, and not really becoming of a future royal; comfortable, if not too elegant, clothes and windswept hairstyle as overblown; altogether, no match for the pencil-slim, demure and occasion-conscious Diana. Already, however, the Fergie image is beginning to settle down. When lively characters give in totally to the staid institution into which they marry, nobody gains. Like Diana, Sarah will find her level, and her public will grow used to it and accept it. These pictures prove she is on her way.

Eleven months after having been given the title Earl of Inverness (in addition to that of Duke of York), it was high time that Prince Andrew paid the revered Scottish town a visit (these pages). Which, in early July of 1987, he did, taking with him his wife who, of course, acquired the title Countess of Inverness on her marriage to him. Unusually, the visit spanned two days, though it was already late afternoon when the royal couple arrived at Dalcross airport to be received by the town's Lord-Lieutenant. A swift evening visit to Queen's Park to open a new spectator stand was as much as there was time for. There were no fewer than nine engagements for the royal couple, if you count the journey they made to the site of the Battle of Culloden, and all of them were carried out in true Scottish style, with husband and wife wearing matching tartan outfits to compliment the dress of the bagpipers who serenaded them on the more formal stages of the visit (above). Fashion watchers noticed that Sarah had merely snipped a few inches off the dress she had worn at the Braemar Games the previous September, but it was the thought that counted. And being a thoughtful couple, they did not forget that they were also Duke and Duchess of York. They called in at York on the way back home, and received the freedom of the city. Unfortunately, many of the good citizens of York who were expected to be there weren't. A blazing sun and soaring temperatures had enticed them away to the seaside!

Ski-ing is not a traditional sport for the British Royal Family, in spite of the now familiar pictures of the Duchess of York (above) and the Princess of Wales (facing page) that grace our newspapers, magazines and television screens each February. Many European royal families have seasoned skiers in their ranks – notably the Dutch, Spanish and Monegasque – but the British royals are comparative latecomers to the slopes. Prince Charles was one of the first of his family to learn the art, back in the early 1960s during a well-publicised holiday with the reigning Prince and Princess of Liechtenstein. He was also one of the first onto the ski-slopes of Europe – neck and neck with the Gloucesters, in fact – establishing a regular British presence in the Swiss Alps by the mid-1970s. The venture has never gone particularly smoothly. The Duchess of Gloucester broke a leg in her earlier years there, and Prince Charles' habit of taking female company – even as part of large mixed parties – to one or other ski resort quickly turned the attention of the media, and resulted in speculation and harassment. 'Go away; you're spoiling my holiday,' became a frequent, despairing cry from the Prince as Europe's photographers assembled to discover and report as much as possible of his lifestyle on these brief winter breaks. Things got so bad that the girlfriends he took there could not handle the publicity, and it was Princess Diana's sister, Lady Sarah Spencer, who felt pressed, probably much against her better judgement, to deny that her ski-ing holiday with him in 1978 was anything more that purely platonic.

When he announced his engagement early in 1981, Prince Charles included ski-ing in the list of things that he and Diana had in common. He had never actually seen her ski, he said, but he was assured she was a very good skier. She had learned the rudiments during her very brief stay at finishing school at the Chateau d'Oex and during a couple of winter sports holidays with friends in the area but, as their early ski-ing forays showed, she was by no means as accomplished as her husband. They spent their first winter sports holiday together in early 1983. It was a disaster in miniature. Naively failing to anticipate at least half an army of photographers, the royal couple were surprised and dismayed by the persistence of press interest in them. It embarrassed their hosts, the Liechtenstein royal family, and embittered the first days of the break. Eventually, the Prince's staff suggested a photocall as a swift and effective means of giving the press what they wanted so that the party could be left in peace. Diana refused to co-operate, refusing her husband's public pleas, and causing him no small degree of perplexed humiliation. On the scent of a front-page 'spoilt-child' story, the photographers continued the daily hunt for the royal skiers, while Diana tried every method to avoid them. Some say she travelled lying on the floor of her car to evade detection, others that she changed cars at national borders, yet others that she used other girls as decoys, dressed in her clothes! Whatever the facts, the whole episode left relations between palace and press tortured and sour. The lessons were learned and, the following year, the royal party dutifully posed and performed a few trial runs that suited the snappers. The holiday went swimmingly, and the Palace couldn't thank the press enough. Things went even better in 1985. Not only was there a prolonged photocall, but Diana was seen actually chatting happily with the photographers, many of whom had been involved in the catastrophe of two years before. More confident of her ski-ing ability, she and Prince Charles made for the higher slopes in a fairly successful attempt to shake off the more persistent

journalists, as well as to improve on their ski-ing experience. Even then, there was a strange interlude in which Diana inexplicably failed to appear after a couple of runs. Charles sent out to look for her everywhere and detectives scoured the area. Eventually the story came back that the Princess had fallen off the ski-lift, and had decided to make for the valley and return to the royal palace at Vaduz by car. Prince Charles, though relieved, was not best pleased. 'I'm the last to know what's going on,' he muttered. A new dimension was introduced the 1986, when Sarah Ferguson joined the royal group, ostensibly as a friend of the Princess, but probably as part of a device to confuse the press over the mounting expectation that she was to be the future Princess Andrew. Surely the Palace would not allow Miss Ferguson to be seen with the Prince and Princess if marriage speculation was to be defused? Nobody knew quite what to expect. In all the confusion, nobody seemed to know either that Sarah was in fact one of the most accomplished skiers in the party. She had been learning since the age of six, when her parents used to take her with them for winter sports, and she had, of course, had the advantage of three years in the Alps during her friendship with Paddy McNally. She was certainly the most stylish performer on skis, and Diana probably learned quite a lot from her during that holiday. On that occasion, the royals forsook their usual Liechtenstein hosts and rented a six-roomed chalet at Wolfgang, near Davos, on the Klosters slopes. The following year, another chalet, nearer Klosters, was taken and both royal couples – Charles, Diana, Andrew and Sarah – were in the party (above). The two ladies had each acquired new ski-suits, Diana's blue-black number with electric pink stripes and matching pink gloves (facing page) proving by far the more chic. For Andrew, whose ski-ing experience goes back to his schooldays at Gordonstoun and Lakeside, Ontario (where he was in the second downhill team), this was the first winter sports holiday for several years.

'She just points herself downhill, and goes,' was how her father described Sarah's ski-ing attitude. He might also have added that she has a penchant for tomfoolery, as everybody discovered during the 1987 photocall. No-one can agree how it happened – either Diana accidentally stood on her ski and Sarah retaliated, or they saw two groups of cameramen jostling for position and decided to imitate them – but soon the two girls were pushing and shoving each other with playful vigour (top) until Diana fell, convulsed with laughter, into the snow. Prince Charles was not amused – 'With these two around, there's no need for me to be here, really,' he remarked – and called them both to order. At least, however, things had changed for the better since the bad old days. The royals got another holiday in peace.

It was the last, probably, for some time. In February 1988, the royal party again arrived at Zurich airport, though not in the snowstorm that characterised the 1986 landing (previous pages right), and were soon posing again for photographs in the foothills, prior to consolidating their ski-ing progress of previous years. The holiday proceeded as normal until, one afternoon, Prince Charles led a small group of friends, Major Hugh Lindsay and Charles and Patti Palmer-Tomkinson, together with a Swiss detective and the Duchess of York's mountain guide, Bruno Sprecher, to an off-piste area of the Klosters slopes for some challenging ski-runs. Their movements started an avalanche of loosened snow further up, and the cascade of ice and snow gathered force and sped past them on its way into the valley. Most of the group managed to avoid the avalanche, but it took two members of it down with it. One of them, Mrs Palmer-Tomkinson, was injured and taken to hospital. The other, Major Lindsay, was struck and killed, probably outright. It brought the holiday to an abrupt and sorrowful end.

The anatomy and analysis of the tragedy at Klosters took almost five months to be determined. An official report by the Swiss authorities confirmed that the royal party's activities had caused the avalanche, but cleared any one of them of actual blame. Its conclusions proved little that was not already known and acknowledged by Prince Charles: he had emphasised within a day of the accident that both he and his friends knew the risks of off-piste ski-ing, that mountains have to be treated with respect, and that no-one is infallible. The personal pain would outlast the report: Mrs Palmer-Tomkinson still in a Swiss hospital, the widowed Mrs Lindsay left to bear the child she was carrying when her husband died, the Prince left to contemplate the curse of sudden and unexpected ill luck, and perhaps that it might even have been worse. There will be new rules for royals on the

slopes from now on. Princess Anne and her family (top and facing page), relative novices to the Alps, and the Kents, who regularly frequent Meribel and Verbieres, where Lady Helen Windsor (top left) is an enthusiastic skier, and the Gloucesters will all have taken the point that, even in their leisure hours, their protection is as vital as when they are on duty and that, in a sense, it is futile for the nation to spend millions of pounds on their security throughout the year only to see their safety put at unacceptable risk on off-duty adventures. At the same time, of course, there have to be compensations for the sheltered, if not somewhat cosseted life, the Royal Family are constrained by their very position, or accident of birth, to lead. The equation is not easy to resolve.

Not many young ladies in their mid-twenties are let into the secrets of modern army warfare. Nor are they invited to walk down lines of cadet soldiers, with the power to inspect every button and shoeshine. They certainly do not enjoy the privilege of five or six trips abroad a year. But for the Princess of Wales, who not so long ago was a kindergarten assistant without a single qualification to her name, all this has become a matter of course. From the time of her momentous wedding to Prince Charles, her gradual initiation into the mysteries of the royal round has evolved under close public scrutiny. It now seems complete and successful, and Diana has long since been able to consider herself a natural at the job. She has travelled the length and breadth of Britain, to most of the countries of Western Europe, to the Middle and Far East, to North America and Australasia. In doing so she has gained presence as well as popularity, to such an extent that we seem a world away from the novelty that pictures such as these would have suggested seven or eight years ago.

Above left: Diana at a school in Qatar during her Gulf tour of 1986, and (above right) at the end of her visit to Spain in the spring of 1987.

Facing page: Diana being shown surveillance equipment during a visit to the 13th/18th Royal Hussars base at Tidworth. Appropriately, she wore a hussar-style outfit when she stood in for the Queen in 1987 at a passing-out parade at Sandhurst (below) at which Prince Paul of Greece passed out as a 2nd Lieutenant in the Royal Dragoon Guards in the presence of his parents and aunt, Queen Sofia of Spain.

Official portraits of Princess Anne as a growing child are virtual period pieces, often depicting her with a sweet, toothy smile and in equally sugary little party frocks. She probably shudders at them now, and blesses the fact that she has a sense of humour. For, in truth, she is nothing like the person projected by those pictures. She is level-headed, business-like and straight-talking, with a healthy scepticism and impatience of pomposity that would make her father proud of her. If she seems tough, it's because she is tough – and that's because, in royal terms at least, she's had tough decisions to make and follow. How she would describe herself, how order the various demands on her time and efforts, is anybody's guess. Wife, mother, horsewoman, charity worker, estate manager, royal globetrotter – who knows which role comes first and for how long? Suffice it to say that she is all of these things, and more, and that she finds time and energy not only to fulfil the claims of each upon her, but also to deal with that persistent media canker that, in a less resolute, more vulnerable person, would eat away at confidence and sense of purpose. With any work-orientated couple, the demands of family and business conflict, and Princess Anne has found that the very separate working lives that she and her husband Mark Phillips lead, and the clear arrangement between them that they do not muscle in on each other's activities, have been interpreted all too often as signs that their marriage is falling apart. Add to that the opportunities for scandal offered by the company each is likely to keep as part of a working lifestyle – secretaries, stable hands, actors and interviewers – and you have all the makings of

misunderstandings, the eternal round of accusation and denial, the blackening of reputations and the strain it puts on a Princess who has devoted twenty years to the service of her own country and of millions of unfortunates beyond its shores.

In a sense, the Phillips family cannot win. Insist that Mark takes part in the royal round, and he becomes a parasite; encourage his absence, and he's failing to support his wife. Allow Anne to spend more time at Gatcombe, and she's wanting to have her cake and eat it; expect a full day's royal work from her, and she's turning her back on her young family. So the no-nonsense Princess adopts a no-nonsense stance: never complain, never explain. Keep plugging away at your three or four hundred royal engagements a year, and do your best for the causes you represent. Maintain your presence in your own right at State occasions, and when that work is done, spend as much time as possible with your family. Engineer no publicity, but let those whose job it is to serve the results up to the public make what they will of it all. Princess Anne has at least once professed a lack of maternal instinct. Yet she has borne two children, presumably out of choice rather than out of duty, and she rarely attends a weekend of horse trials without taking them with her. Both Peter and Zara are enthusiastic and accomplished for their ages, and Zara in particular is a dedicated learner under her mother's instruction as (above) at a gymkhana, as well as a keen spectator each year at Windsor (facing page).

Middle East politics make British State or official visits to the area a delicate matter, but the Royal Family have more than once ventured into this diplomatic arena and succeeded. In one such foray at the end of 1986, the Prince and Princess of Wales spent nine days visiting Oman, Bahrein, Qatar and Saudi Arabia. Social customs were also difficult to get used to. The society of these countries is heavily male-orientated, and Diana found herself left out of many of the meetings in which, in a Western society, she would have joined her husband as a matter of course. Nevertheless, the settings were splendid: a full-scale guard of honour at Bahrein (below) and a palatial meeting with the Amir of Qatar (bottom) emphasised the importance of this first major royal visit since the Queen's in 1979. For Diana, it was a time to compromise between her Western fashions and the demands of Middle Eastern modesty. All her day dresses, such as the one she wore on arrival in Saudi Arabia (facing page) were much longer than usual, and specifically designed so that, once the tour was over, they could be taken up and used again back home.

The four days in Oman were typical of the restrictions Diana had to live with for the privilege of experiencing a fascinating tour such as this. Although the Sultan of Oman is a great friend of Britain and a close acquaintance of the Royal Family, he hosted his guests in a way which accorded fairly strictly with Omani customs. Much of her time was spent in harems where, while Prince Charles attended meetings with sheiks and politicians, she chatted for hours with women who explained to her, for instance, how brides-to-be were escorted to bed, to remain there for the whole of the day before their weddings. Worse still, Diana found that even going for a swim in the palace pool was something she had to do when Charles was not around. And perhaps the most famous incident happened when she presented Prince

Charles with a trophy after he had scored in a local polo match. As she always does, she planted a big kiss on his cheek as she handed the prize over – and then found that the scene was edited out of the television report that evening! For other reasons, the visit to Qatar did not go too smoothly either. Not only was Diana excluded from receptions with the Amir (overleaf left top), but a visit to a desert camel race proved a let-down when the royal couple, seen arriving (above) discovered that the races were taking place virtually out of sight of the tent, and the long, desultory conversations within (facing page top) left Diana feeling occasionally bored (overleaf left bottom). She was also distressed by the rough treatment some of the camels received from their handlers.

Things improved in Bahrein, where Diana's concern for handicapped children was recognised. She was taken to one of the capital's homes for the handicapped (facing page bottom left), where she was presented with a sumptuous scarlet and gold traditional dress. And, as a special concession, the Emir actually allowed her to attend the State banquet he gave for Prince Charles' 38th birthday that day. But it was the Saudi Arabians who provided the final flourish. Their camel race was one which their visitors could see, and in which Diana was invited by Prince Sultan, second in line to the throne, to present the trophies (previous pages left bottom) She was well looked after during the entire three-day trip (facing page: top right and bottom right) by Prince Saud Faud, and the Saudis actually provided cutlery for the royal couple to eat their whole roast sheep with – normally the meat is just torn apart by hand. At one stage, they discreetly slipped a black briefcase into Diana's hand: inside it she found a telephone and an invitation to phone home to speak to William and Harry!

The Queen is no great devotee of nights out: rumour has it that she'd rather spend her evenings watching television or doing jigsaw puzzles. So it is something of a coup for any charity to secure her attendance at a gala occasion laid on for its benefit. And it gives the rest of us a chance of seeing her at her most regal. Top: meeting comedian Les Dawson at the 1987 Royal Variety Performance, (above) at the premiere of *Melba* at the West End's Cannon Cinema, (top right) fun and games at the Albert Hall in 1985, and (right) arriving for a charity showing of *White Knights* in Leicester Square. Facing page: other royal spectaculars, including (top) Princess Anne at Sadler's Wells Ballet, (bottom right) the Duchess of Gloucester at a Guildhall banquet for the King and Queen of Spain and (bottom left) Prince Philip with the King of Norway on his State Visit.

The Japanese are noted for their efficiency, a quality which obliges them to pack as many engagements as possible into any day of a royal visit. The Queen discovered this in the mid-1970s, and Prince Charles and Princess Diana discovered it again a decade later. After an exhausting visit to Canada, where Diana had fainted at the Vancouver Expo, it seemed unlikely that she would stay the course – but she did! Tactfully, she chose a striking red-and-white outfit reminiscent of the Japanese national flag for her arrival and visit to the royal guest pavilion at Kyoto (top left). Then the royal couple were hosted at a tea ceremony (left) at Nijo Castle, the ritual taking only fifteen minutes of precious royal time instead of the usual ninety. Afterwards, Diana received a couple of kimonos, and delighted her guests by actually trying one on (facing page). A typical busy day in Tokyo saw Diana visiting a Red Cross Hospital, a television studio, a department store (top) and the Yushin Tei Pavilion, where she watched an exhibition of doll making and flower arranging. All of which was followed by a banquet at the British Embassy at which she was escorted by the Emperor's grandson, Prince Hiro (above), a former student at Oxford University.

Despite appearances, it's probably true that no commoner has married into the Royal Family without some apprehension. Princess Diana admitted that, though she initially had no doubts, she found the job very difficult. Nevertheless, the Duchess of York threw herself into the royal round with gusto. Her expansive, sometimes theatrical dress sense, as seen at a Mansion House reception (below) at the Savoy (below right), at the Royal Variety Performance (bottom left) and at the premiere of *Beverly Cop II* in October 1987 (facing page) in this amazing Zandra Rhodes evening dress, matches her confidence, giving the impression that she will arrive in her own way. And, to prove her sense of humour, this (bottom right) was the way she arrived at Heathrow Airport recently to see off a group of handicapped children on a Disneyworld holiday.

The role of royalty outside the constitutional functions vested in the Crown is probably best summed up in these pictures, taken within two days of each other, shortly after the Queen's return from the Australian bicentennial celebrations in May 1988. Above and facing page bottom pictures: she attends a reception at St James's Palace to mark the tenth anniversary of Motability, the charity organisation that helps physically disabled people get around. Here the Queen hands over keys of specially built or adapted cars to disabled motorists and their families. Motability is a young charity, and the Queen's public support for it on this anniversary gives it a sudden promotional benefit which is probably worth as much as a substantial fund-raising operation. Facing page top: a quite different royal function is illustrated – the Queen acting out one of the traditional ceremonial events

that punctuate a more routine royal schedule with colour and ritual. Here, with Prince Philip and her 86-year-old aunt, Princess Alice, Duchess of Gloucester, she arrives at St Paul's Cathedral for a service for the Order of the British Empire. The ceremony, a cross between a thanksgiving and a re-dedication to the cause of public service for which its members have been admitted to the Order, is rich in symbolism, and to many people may seem antiquated and irrelevant. But it recalls, at least in some measure, the historical basis from which our society, for better or worse, developed, and keeps alive the sense of public obligation which those in the more privileged positions of our present, unequal society, should observe in favour of the less fortunate.

The Queen Mother is the nation's Granny – she knows it, and rather revels in it. A grandmother of six and great-grandmother of five, she now glides towards her tenth decade basking in the warmth of a nation's guaranteed affections, while a visit to the gates of Clarence House on any August 4th should convince any sceptic of the gentle strength of this smiling dowager's hold over her public of almost seventy years. Much has been made of the tragedies of her life, but the overall story has been of sunshine and success. Her husband's early death through cancer, now known to have been brought on by heavy smoking, her younger daughter's volatile personal life, and the gnawing bitterness of the Windsor saga, are all probably outweighed by the serenity and public adoration which have blessed almost forty years of widowhood. She shines on duty as no other member of her family shines, and her wartime identification with ordinary Cockneys is still reflected in her public engagements: (below) at St Martin-in-the-Fields where, during the war, she joined audiences for lunchtime recitals; and (left and bottom) with the Pearlies during the 900th anniversary celebrations of the church that gave us the legend of Bow Bells.

In contrast, Princess Margaret has not been so successful in capturing the affections of the British people who, though they tend to approve a vibrant character, prefer that it should be suitably restrained. It is not an easy combination of requirement, and the Princess has long since abandoned the policy of keeping up appearances that do not reflect her choices in life. Undoubtedly wounded by the Establishment-led crushing of her first true love, let down by the ultimate failure of her marriage, rocked by the rawness of the scandals that pursued her extravagant Caribbean lifestyle and persistent private friendships, and possibly dismayed by recent health setbacks, she has followed her own course and allowed the public to follow theirs. In many ways, this is a tragedy in its own right. Young in outlook, she belies her approach to her 60th birthday with every public appearance. The glamorous aspects of her existence, such as the annual Caledonian Ball (this page) in London, show an unabashed love of the high life and fun, both on duty and off. But she is also a person of great culture and talent, with a lifelong interest in good causes such as the NSPCC and the Girl Guide Association, and a restored sense of public duty which, alas, has in recent years gone virtually unnoticed by a press with other fish to fry.

Australia's government is not too favourably inclined towards royalty at present, but Bicentennial Year made it aware of certain priorities. No fewer than eight members of the Royal Family visited there in 1988, and none more keen than Charles and Diana. 'If it takes regular visitors from an old country to help you decide whether or not you should be celebrating,' the Prince told an Australia Day audience in Sydney, 'my wife and I will be glad to be of assistance'. Diana, dressed in one of her favourite outfits (facing page) looked delighted to be back for her third major visit, and throughly enjoyed the carnival atmosphere as she and Prince Charles were taken out by boat (bottom) into Sydney's huge natural harbour where the flotilla of tall ships (below) made their triumphal way past the Opera House and under the Harbour Bridge.

Top pictures: two contrasting studies of Diana; (right) looking elegant and well-groomed while meeting guests at a reception in Adelaide, and (left) the carefree, casual look on board the inspection boat on that breezy trip round Sydney Harbour. The smile hides the effect of a recent scare: one of the thousands of boats in the harbour came rather too close before letting off its official naval gun salute. The Princess jumped back, visibly alarmed, and it took her and her lady-in-waiting several moments to recover their composure. Earlier, Diana got lost among the ranks of soldiers who formed the Guard of Honour on their arrival at the Sydney waterfront, and she had to slip nimbly between two guardsmen in order to join Prince Charles, who was carrying out the inspection. No visit by Charles and Diana to Australia seems complete without a display of their dancing capabilities, and this tour proved no exception. This time, the venue was Melbourne, whose traditionally conservative upper crust were treated to a whirling example of Forties Swing. Unceremoniously hitching up the bodice of a superb dress by Catherine Walker of the Chelsea Design Company, said to cost upwards of £800, Diana footed it with Charles (facing page) to the tune of Glenn Miller's *In The Mood*. As always on these occasions, Charles proved a little too enthusiastic, and the royal party-piece was momentarily interrupted as his wife told him to 'steady on'. Eventually, she waved her invitation to the other guests to join them on the floor, which soon became jammed with couples wanting to rub shoulders, literally, with the royals.

After travelling to Melbourne and Adelaide, the royal couple returned to Sydney, again in the blazing heat for which Australian Januarys are famous, which explains why the Queen prefers to arrange her many visits during the cooler months between March and October. A sunny walkabout in Sydney allowed Diana to make the most of a colourful, lightweight outfit (above), while the more intense coastal heat of the shoreline north of Sydney prompted her to wear even simpler clothes (facing page). This occasion, normally an annual lifesaving parade and series of competitions, was officially dubbed the Bicentennial Surf Carnival, and the afternoon reached its climax when the royal Landrover convoy glided over the sand (facing page bottom) to take the Prince and Princess to their vantage points. Perhaps 'glided' is not quite the right word, since one of the vehicles became stuck when its wheels caught in a length of rope: to ironic cheers from the large crowd, it had to be pushed on by hand. All of which added substantially to the fun of things. Shaded from an unrelenting sun by canvas awning, Prince Charles quaffed beer while his wife sipped an orange cooler, and both watched hours of boisterous activity intended to display the best of Australian manliness and skill. For the winning team there was a prize, newly minted under the impressive title 'The Prince and Princess of Wales Trophy'. And, with all that beefcake around, who better to present it than the 'bonzer sheila' herself. At least, she didn't seem to take exception to the idea (facing page top).

If you were ever to ask Diana for examples of her favourite and least favourite duties, she might well point to two contrasts that Australia 1988 offered. At Woollongong, she attended a Town Hall reception at which she had to shake hands with all of 500 guests. Not a physically demanding job, but one that invites boredom of the most chronic kind, despite surface smiles (facing page). Take her to a kindergarten like the Roy Caughey Centre for Needy Families in Auburn, however, and she will throw herself into the fun and simple rewards of working with children. 'It's just heaven to get back among children again,' she said, and her reactions to the attentions of little Trudy (below) say it all.

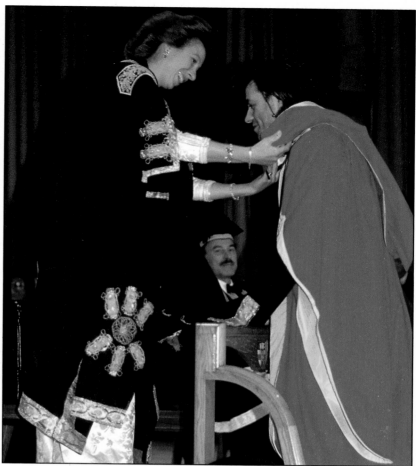

No-one gave serious credence to the possibility that Princess Anne would be given – or rather, would accept – the title of Princess Royal. Though traditionally bestowed upon the sovereign's eldest daughter, it seemed dour and spinsterly, too often associated with silver-haired, elderly aunts. The fact that Anne not only accepted it, but has made it mean something, shows that she is not overwhelmed by family history, for nothing could be more different than her direct, down-to-earth attitude, and the more genteel, perhaps dullish image of the title's former holders. The title was also seen as the Queen's acknowledgement of her only daughter's fantastic contribution to public life. Strange to think that, just a few years ago she was considered arrogant, presumptuous and rude – the result of the continual contretemps with the press, usually when she wanted no more than to put her horses through their competitive paces in peace. Now, after years of devotion to the Save the Children Fund, and an engagement schedule second in intensity only to those of her parents, she enjoys public favour as well as her mother's lasting appreciation of her worth to the family firm. Those engagements cover a wide spectrum of activities: charitable, with a visit to the Butler Trust in London in March 1987 (facing page) and attendance of the charity premiere of the film *Absolute Beginners* (top left); educational, as when, as Chancellor of London University (a post she has held since the Queen Mother retired in 1980), she conferred an honorary Doctorate of Science and Economics on Bob Geldof (top right) for his famine relief work; and regimental – a uniformed Princess inspecting the Royal Marines (above).

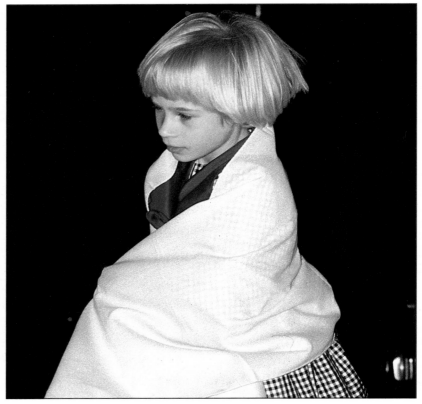

The Gloucester family have always opted for a quiet life by royal standards, and have achieved a public profile consistent with a peaceful pursuit of family life. Their senior member is Princess Alice (above), one of the Queen's two surviving aunts, and only sixteen months the Queen Mother's junior. Despite her years, she belies her admission that she is 'failing in sight and limbs', and has for years found it difficult to bow out of public life. Her only surviving son, the Duke of Gloucester, is now in his mid-forties and combines a modicum of royal duties with his chosen career as an architect.

His Danish-born wife, noted for her unaffected charm and fetching dress sense, has borne him three children: Alexander, Earl of Ulster; Lady Davina Windsor, seen (right) with the Princess of Wales; and Lady Rose Windsor (above). Top: the Duchess of Gloucester at the premiere of the film *Pavlova* in London in 1985, and (facing page bottom right) at the Sir Robert Mayer Memorial Concert at the Barbican. Facing page top right: Princess Alice, her son and daughter-in-law at the Albert Hall for the Festival of Remembrance.

'I grew too tall,' explains Diana, whenever she is asked why she gave up ballet lessons as a teenager. But she has never lost touch, and the Royal London Ballet was one of the first organisations of its kind to secure her patronage. In May 1988 she visited the Royal Ballet School (top left and facing page) and watched, no doubt nostalgically, youngsters as they displayed their knowledge and grasp of the dance. Facing page: (bottom) planting a commemorative shrub in the School's grounds, and (top) leaving by car afterwards. Top right: a beaming Princess of Wales arriving at the London Coliseum for a performance of *The Magic Flute*, in aid of the National Hospital for Nervous Diseases. More tight-lipped, she prepares to make a speech (above) as she opens a new leisure pool at Sheringham in Norfolk, and points without comment to the crowd of photographers behind her (right) as she leaves a reception to mark the 25th year of the National Children's Bureau.

Lady Helen Windsor (facing page) is one of four royal children born within two months of each other – a run of events which gave 1964 the title of 'The Year of the Royal Babies'. She is the second of the three children of the Duke of Kent, a cousin of the Queen, who in 1961 married Miss Katharine Worsley, the daughter of the Lord Lieutenant for the then North Riding of Yorkshire. The Duke of Kent (seen (bottom) with his wife and daughter at a christening party given by the King and Queen of Greece for their fifth child Prince Philippos in 1986), is another essentially low-profile royal, rarely prominent except in connection with export drives, regimental duties (which recall his long military career) and the All England Lawn Tennis Championships at Wimbledon. This annual event owes much of its royal patronage to Queen Mary and to her daughter-in-law Princess Marina, who was President of the All England Club until her death in 1968, when the Duke took over. His wife, the present Duchess, is also a keen tennis devotee, and is to be seen during most of Wimbledon's thirteen days of championships (left) along with other royal tennis watchers, including the Princess of Wales (below), whose informal tennis match with 1988 ladies champion Steffi Graf became instant news.

The education of kings-to-be is a gamble. Prince Charles didn't much like his, and hopes his son will fare better. So palace nursery traditions have been broken and, at three, young Wills went to a Kensington kindergarten. He looked none too thrilled (right) but the experiment brought him into early contact with others, and prepared him for his first school – Wetherby's, where cousin Freddie Windsor had done well. Diana was confident, on leaving him there (above) on that first morning in January 1987, that all was well, and both headmistress Miss Blair-Turner (facing page bottom left) and William (facing page top right) seemed happy with the first day's work. Holidays and weekends are still more fun, with polo visits (facing page bottom right), riding (top right) and the chance to pretend you're a police outrider (top) or a fireman (facing page top left).

It's no secret that the British and Spanish royal families have formed a mutual admiration society. There is every reason for this, not least that Elizabeth II and Juan Carlos I are third cousins. So, despite the little matter of the Spanish king's boycott of Charles and Diana's wedding because the newlyweds were to pass through Gibraltar, it is inevitable that the two families should occasionally want to see more of each other. It happens almost every year, as in April 1987 (these pages), when the Waleses paid a four-day semi-official visit to Spain. The king's twin daughters, Cristina and Elena, met them in Madrid (bottom), where they were joined by Juan Carlos and Queen Sofia (sister of the exiled Greek King Constantine). That evening a family banquet in the Zarzuela Palace (below and right) included local asparagus and sole, chocolate soufflé, fruit slices and a selection of Spain's fifty regional cheeses. In the following two days, the visitors enjoyed tours of the superb Prado art gallery, Toledo's Gothic cathedral and Salamanca University (where Diana performed a ritual walk over students' gowns); swam in the Spanish king's palace pool; called in at a night-club in Madrid's historic quarter, and were jostled by crowds in a market, where Diana eventually bought some ceramic tableware. A busy, eventful visit which ended with genuinely effusive farewells (facing page).

There was much talk of a second honeymoon as the Duke and Duchess of York left London at the end of September 1987 for a five-day official trip to the Indian Ocean island of Mauritius, but it was quickly stamped on. News filtered through that Andrew's old ship, HMS *Brazen*, was due to dock there, and that he was arranging a couple of boisterous reunion parties for his former shipmates. When the royal couple arrived at Port Louis, they were greeted by a sharp breeze which lifted the Duchess' skirt (left), consequent wolf-whistles, and garlands of frangipani and anthurium – the island's national flower.

The visit was a riot of sunshine, colour and good humour. The Duchess bubbled with excitement at the local racecourse (above), where she and the Duke watched the Duke of York Stakes, and poked fun at him for having backed the wrong horse. She planted a spice tree in the grounds of a former sugar plantation so enthusiastically that her low-cut dress revealed rather too much: when, the next day (left), she was asked to help Prince Andrew plant another commemorative tree, she told pressmen that she was not going to give them another front page picture, thank you very much! At Pamplemousse (facing page) the couple visited the site of a new cardiac ward at the National Hospital, then watched a yacht race sitting on the deck of a trimaran. Most evenings gave the Duchess a chance to sparkle in evening dress (top) with Government banquets, Embassy receptions and high society dinners.

For one of her very earliest evening outings with Prince Charles after her engagement, Princess Diana wore a low-cut black gown described then as 'daring'. Although our capacity for saucy surprises has since narrowed, the dress certainly revealed rather more than she may have intended, especially when her exit from the royal Rolls entailed a fair degree of body stoop. Casual observers thought she had gone too far too soon, while more serious fashion-watchers wondered what she could ever do to better the effect. In the years since, however, Diana has rarely looked back. Despite spasms of modesty, she has never forsaken the dramatic allure of the plunging neckline. The difference now is that she makes news, not because of what she does, or may, reveal, but for her stunning presentation. The imaginative shoulder strap topping the black dress which she wore (left) for the premiere of *Out of Africa* make the style positively regal, while the slightly more showy evening wear she chose (above) for the 1988 premiere of *The Last Emperor* echoed the richness of the last courts of imperial China.

For one who is, by all accounts, a very private person, essentially reserved, makes friends none too easily, and enjoys virtually solitary pleasures (bottom right), the Queen does lead a remarkably outgoing public life. We often forget, as we witness her often unspontaneous public performance, listen to her strained speeches and watch her stifled reactions to even the most spectacular show staged in her honour, that she is not a natural performer, not a born speaker and certainly not one to respond to order. Public duties of the range and intensity that she undertakes thus impose upon her a considerable weight of effort which her experience lets us take for granted. The yellow outfit (facing page), for instance, reminds us that she first wore it for a week-long visit to China which entailed a heavy schedule, and the continual effort of responding to the unspoken demands of a

government and society whose precepts and sense of priorities are very different from our own. At home, too, she is almost by custom put into some strange positions. A visit to Henley-on-Thames sees her travelling (below left) by motor launch, surrounded by officials and escorted by uniformed watermen: hardly the circumstances for relaxed, natural behaviour. By custom, too, she pays an annual visit to the Chelsea Flower Show (bottom left), despite having little real interest in or ability at gardening. And perhaps, though surrounded by family, politicians, statesmen, the Church and her own Household Brigades, she never feels more lonely than when, each November, she stands (below) for those long, sombre two minutes of silence to lead the nation in homage to the dead of two world wars.

Right: the Duke and Duchess of York arriving at Cowes on the Royal Yacht *Britannia*, shortly after their wedding: they had spent their honeymoon in the Azores aboard the yacht. Flowers were a big theme of the Yorks' wedding, with festoons of them draping the pillars of Westminster Abbey, so it was natural that the new royal Patron of the National Association of Flower Arranging should be presented with an especially attractive basket of flowers (below) when she arrived in Jersey, the island of flowers. Below right: making friends with the Chelsea Pensioners; Sarah becomes the latest royal to take on the annual review of the old soldiers at Chelsea Royal Hospital in June 1987. By the end of that month she was enjoying the thrills of championship tennis (bottom right) at Wimbledon, an occasion attended at one time or another during Wimbledon fortnight by almost all members of the Royal Family, with the notable exceptions of the Queen, Prince Philip and the Prince of Wales.

Facing page: a variety of moods for the Duchess. She was back from honeymoon in time to help the Queen Mother (herself Duchess of York from 1923 to 1936) celebrate her 86th birthday at Clarence House (bottom left). She soon stamped her character on her in-laws, and by the following year was blazing the trail for the controversial royal participation in It's A Knockout: (top left) Sarah arriving at Alton Towers for the competition. A hint of things to come (top right) as she inspects a premature baby in an incubator during a visit to a Cardiff maternity hospital. Bottom right: a sad homecoming as Sarah and Diana leave the aircraft that brought them back from Switzerland, following the death of their friend, Major Hugh Lindsay, in the avalanche that abruptly ended their ski-ing holiday.

It may seem a dull idea to spend three days pushing British exports abroad, but when the royals are involved, there is no lack of spectacle. In April 1986, the Prince and Princess of Wales went to Vienna as part of a 'Britain in Vienna' trade drive, and both the city and its royal visitors experienced the best of each other. Vienna's gift of a model of a Lippizaner riding stallion on the arrival of the Prince and Princess (right) may have given the impression that Austria has exports to sell too, but the purpose of the visit was re-established by the royal gift of a very British piece of Brierley crystal in return. There was a carriage drive through the Union Jack-bedecked streets to the presidential palace, a visit to an exhibition of the best of British design

and fine art, and a gala performance of Congreve's comedy *Love for Love*, performed by the London National Theatre, at which Princess Diana wore this shimmering, turquoise dress (above). She displayed a quieter elegance for the official banquet at the Rathaus (right), a line she followed on the final day when she visited the Vienna Boys Choir school (top), where she was proudly welcomed with a madrigal sung by over fifty of the boys. One of them was lucky enough to present her with her bouquet (facing page). It wasn't the only gift: she also brought back a couple of pairs of lederhosen for the children.

Prince Charles has probably never struck anybody as an aggressive, far less warlike, character. Royal traditions, however, die hard and, as he is next in line not only to the Throne but also the post of Commander in Chief of the armed forces, his occasional identification with the military and understanding of their work is required. And, being obedient to duty above all, he meets that requirement. This fortunately does not come hard. He has been linked with the services since 1970. He has flown jet aircraft, learned to parachute, gained his wings. He has commanded a mine-sweeper, served on guided missile destroyers and frigates. He passed an assault course at Lympstone, and one gets the feeling that he would not have opted out of the Marines. When he left the Navy after five years' service, he was better qualified and far more experienced in real terms than any Prince of Wales in a relative position. His brother Andrew has joked that Charles has medals on his chest that don't mean a thing, but the probability is that, had the need arisen, he would have more than proved himself in the defence of the realm. The Army was never his preferred career, but it does not prevent him from lending his patronage in the shape of numerous Colonelcies in Chief and, more important, regular visits to his regiments in Europe and around the world. Nor are these visits merely cosmetic. In 1986 he turned up in uniform to see how the Parachute Regiment was coping with the delicate job of

maintaining a presence on the border between Greek and Turkish sectors on Cyprus (facing page, bottom right). And on his visits to troops based in Germany, such as (above and top) in Paderborn with the 5th Royal Inniskillens and (remaining pictures) with the Royal Regiment of Wales, he acquires experience of potential life in the front line, manoeuvring tanks and aiming their guns, and loading and firing rocket launchers (right).

Prince Michael of Kent was something of a royal unknown until in 1978 he married the sparkling, beautiful Baroness Marie-Christine von Reibnitz. The marriage was controversial then, because the lady was a divorcee and Catholic; Prince Michael had to seek the Queen's permission to marry (which she gave) and renounce his rights of succession to the Throne (which he did). The marriage has also been controversial since, with accusations that the Princess was something of a social climber, penny-pinching, too forceful for the Royal Family's liking. While these journalistic darts continued to be thrown, mostly without evidence in support, she suffered her worst setback when it became known that her father had been a member of the German SS. She denied any personal knowledge of this, and that therefore her duty to reveal the fact to the Queen at the time of her marriage was ever an issue. The intensity of the public debate was so fierce that she broke down in tears while speaking at a public function, but it did little to staunch the media's opprobrium. Another accusation, this time that she had had an affair with a Texas oil millionaire, followed. Though it was fairly successfully deflected, the Princess then did herself few favours by giving an interview on U.S. television in which she said that she only went to charity functions, like the White Dove Ball at the Dorchester Hotel (facing page, bottom right) out of a sense of duty, and never enjoyed them. 'They bore me rigid,' she said; a statement which proved to many that she had surely gone too far. Since when, all has been quiet. She and Prince Michael are busy bringing up their two children Freddie (facing page, bottom left) and Ella (left) and undertaking public duties, such as this visit to a fashion show at the Victoria and Albert Museum (facing page, top), by choice, since they do not receive payment from Civil List funds. Both are active equestrians, and are to be seen at éventing grounds – (below) at Badminton in 1985 – around the country.

Sovereigns around the world enjoy celebrating their birthdays, and the King of Thailand is no exception. He therefore invited the Prince and Princess of Wales to help celebrate his sixtieth in February 1988. The visit was essentially informal, and made-to-measure for the tourist. No ordinary tourists, these, however, judging by the huge umbrellas, mauve coloured, symbolising exclusive royal use (bottom right) as the Prince and Princess arrived at Bangkok; or by the flower petals strewn in their way in one of the city's parks (below); or by the superlative evening dress the Princess wore (right) at a dinner in honour of her and her husband. Even at an umbrella factory (bottom) in Chang Mai province, one sample was six times normal size, and bore the greeting: 'A warm welcome to Her Royal Highness the Princess of Wales.'

Two highlights marked this comparatively short tour. One was the Prince and Princess' visit to the Temple of the Emerald Buddha, the reverential heart of Bangkok combining the sanctuary of respect and fealty towards the ancient Thai monarchy with the focus of Buddhist worship. After admiring the precincts (bottom) the royal couple went inside without removing their shoes, under a dispensation granted by the King to honoured guests. A leisurely afternoon began with a river trip by launch (below). Then came the second highlight: a magnificent dinner at the Grand Palace, hosted by the Crown Prince of Thailand. It was an evening of compromises: the hosts kept the spices to a minimum to suit the guests' palates, while Diana wore exotic colours and fabrics, and put a lotus flower, Thailand's national symbol, in her hair.

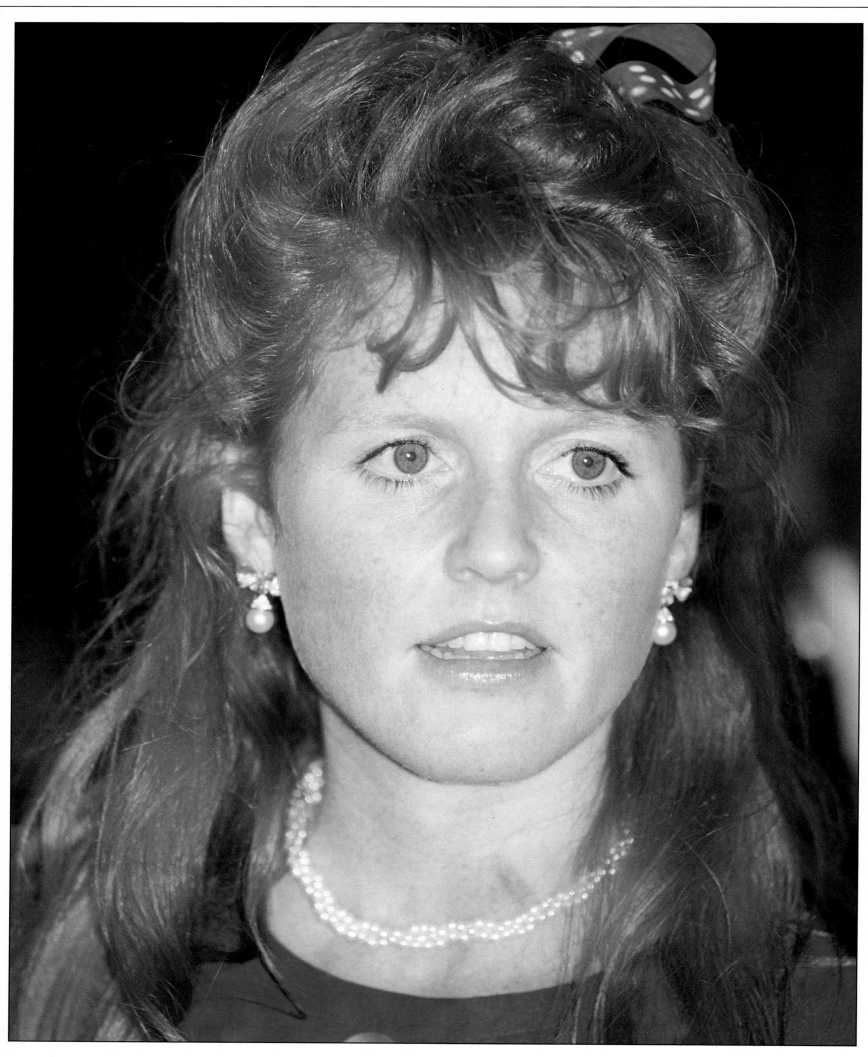

It is interesting to reflect how different our attitudes have been towards the Princess of Wales and the Duchess of York. These two pictures, taken in Jersey (above) and at King's College Hospital in London (facing page) show her at her most pensive, yet even here she does not seem remotely as vulnerable, and certainly not as shy, as Diana in her early royal days. So, whereas public reaction tended to be protective, sometimes obsessively so, towards Diana, it has been decidedly less so towards the girl whose original press nickname of Fergie was itself almost a symbol of her ability to look after herself. Prince Andrew once jokingly referred to her as 'wild and woolly', and she, also jokingly, nearly throttled him in public for his pains. It convinced anyone who still had doubts, that she needs no protection from us!

Facing page: when the wife of Paddy Whiteland, Diana's caretaker and handyman at Highgrove, died in 1986, the Princess attended the family funeral (top left). An unusual gesture for members of the Royal Family, who are often represented by others at funerals and memorial services, Diana's presence signified great personal friendship with the couple, who had looked after Highgrove ever since the Prince and Princess took it over in 1981.

Happier days that year in Hampshire, when the Princess visited the Royal Hampshire Regiment at Winchester (bottom right) and again at Tidworth (top right) to present new colours. Bottom left: an onlooker takes a quick snap for the family album as Diana visits the National Maritime Museum at Greenwich. This page: the Princess visiting the Royal Air Force Hospital at Ely in 1987.

Facing page: as Patron of the British Lung Foundation, Diana is a frequent visitor to hospitals where research work is being carried out. This visit (top left) was to Brompton Hospital in London, not far from where she used to share a flat before her marriage. Another personal connection leads her to re-visit St Mary's Hospital, Paddington, as she did in 1986 (top right), where both her children were born. Bottom left: a visit to Clerkenwell and (bottom right) to Dundee, both in the same year. This page: some of Diana's more striking daytime outfits. A warm two piece worn at Ascot – and again in Bonn – in 1987 (top); a military-style suit for the 1987 Sandhurst parade (above); a slim, stylish coat-dress in Madrid that year (right), and a boldly-striped outfit for her visit to a flower festival in Ely (top right).

For a pageant to mark the 650th anniversary of the Duchy of Cornwall in 1987, a smiling Princess Diana accompanied Prince Charles to the small town of Trewithen (top). More smiles on two hospital visits that year: (above) at Maida Vale Hospital in North London, as Patron of the National Hospital for Nervous Diseases and (right) visiting the Princess Anne Hospital in Southampton to open a new research laboratory funded by the British Lung Foundation of which Diana is Patron, and to see research projects in progress. Shortly after the hurricane that devastated much of the south and southeast of Britain, Diana paid a visit to Sevenoaks (top right), which lost six of the oak trees that gave the town its name. Facing page: the Princess arriving at the American Institute for Foreign Study in 1988 to open a new student centre.

The worst disfavour you can accord a loyal Scot is to call his sovereign the Queen of England. Not all Scots bear heartfelt allegiance to what they regard as an absentee monarch, but those who do are tenacious in their loyalties. Keeping these loyalties afloat means that continual royal journeys north of the border are made each year. The Queen and Duke of Edinburgh spend a full week or more in Scotland every summer, and take up residence in the Palace of Holyroodhouse for the duration. They also, with as many members of the family as possible, attend the annual Braemar Games early in September – one of the few duties they perform during their high summer holiday at Balmoral. It's a festival that Queen Victoria began to patronise almost a century and a half ago, and which even the latest member of the family, the Duchess of York, attended on her return from honeymoon in 1986 (top right). By contrast, the Queen Mother is an old hand here and is seen (facing page, top left) arriving with Prince Charles 1987, during a holiday which also takes in a short visit to her old childhood home at Glamis Castle. Facing page, bottom left: the Yorks on one of their earliest joint visits to Scotland in 1986; (above) at Ballater, near Balmoral, that year; on the first day (facing page, bottom right) and second day (facing page, top right) of their two-day visit to Inverness in 1987. Top left: the Princess of Wales on the Isle of Bute.

Perhaps the most frequent remarks made about Princess Anne's two children are (a) that they are mischievous and (b) that they are not really royal at all. Perhaps (b) explains (a). It is true that, although both Peter (above) and Zara (facing page) are in line to the Throne – respectively eighth and ninth – their mother's marriage to a commoner denies them royal status. But they are very much part of the family. Peter was a pageboy, and Zara a bridesmaid, at Uncle Andrew's wedding in 1986, and both featured in the charming family photograph, issued to mark the royal ruby wedding in November 1987, showing the Queen and Prince Philip with their four grandchildren. The Phillips' children's reputation for mischief probably grew from the repeated sight of Anne and Mark giving them a good wigging at Badminton for bad behaviour: the most famous example of this culminated in a sound walloping in front of the cameras. It shouldn't happen again: Peter will soon be leaving prep school for Marlborough, where mischief is not tolerated too well. And Zara herself will doubtless be at public school in her turn in 1992.

It has long since been inevitable that the ladies of the Royal Family are regarded as leaders – or at least approvers – of fashion trends. Most of them would claim to be no such thing, but the Princess of Wales would be hard put to deny that many of her schemes either establish fashions or set the royal seal of approval onto them. Before her arrival on the scene, for instance, the customary royal decoration around the neck was a double or treble row of pearls, or a jewelled necklace from among the royal heirlooms. Diana has changed all that, and shown that royal customs do not have to be

followed slavishly. At the premiere of *Superman* (above), for instance, she wore no jewellery round her neck, but let this ice-blue, matching chiffon scarf complement her evening dress. At another premiere (facing page), she reverted to an old favourite, the choker. Reminiscent of Edwardian times, this is worn high on the neck, which allows the patterned gauze across the bodice of the dress to the seen to full effect, without interruption from pendulous jewellery.

Trooping the Colour – the ceremonial celebration of the Queen's official birthday – is the highlight of the royal season, and the most unchanging of all British traditions. Or so it seems. There have in fact been numerous modifications to the hour-long ritual since it began life as a birthday tribute in the eighteenth century. The latest of these occurred in 1987, when Burmese, the police mare that carried the Queen to and from the parade for almost two decades, was finally retired. The Queen decided that she did not want to break in a replacement horse and that, she herself being in her early sixties, now might be the time to opt for a more comfortable mode of transport. Hence the elegant barouche which now (previous page and facing page) bowls down the Mall on the second Saturday of June. With this change, the familiar old ceremony has lost something. The sight of the

monarch in full military uniform, riding side-saddle to join her troops on parade, and to lead them from Horse Guards afterwards, was impressive and unique. Now, there is no occasion on which the Queen, as Commander-in-Chief of her Army, wears its uniform, and the sight of the sovereign in day-dress surveying the scene from her low-slung carriage seat is one of a lonely, vulnerable woman. But the other annual joys remain: a special cheer for the Queen Mother, whose own little procession, with two or three other members of the family (above), precedes her daughter's; the balcony scene (top), with its substantial complement of royals; and a noisy RAF flypast, bringing a sense of wonder and delight to even the tiniest watchers (overleaf).

Princess Anne has been President of the Save the Children Fund for some eighteen years. In the last seven, she has put her presidency to practical use by carrying out numerous fact-finding, morale-boosting tours to distressed and under-privileged corners of the world – and has done her public image a power of good into the bargain. One of the most newsworthy of her recent expeditions was that which followed the alarming public realisation, in December 1984, that large tracts of the Sudan were on the verge of almost terminal famine. In the wake of the world relief programme that followed,

Princess Anne rounded off a twenty-three-day African tour with a week-long visit to the Sudan. Two days were spent in Khartoum, where she attended a reception on her arrival (facing page, top), and visited the capital's Children's Hospital (facing page, bottom) to see how a typical urban medical centre copes with its workload. Then she took to the famine-stricken provinces, and saw how a far more dire problem was being tackled. On-the-spot information, such as was given in a tent at Umbala (above) was sought, and welcomed.

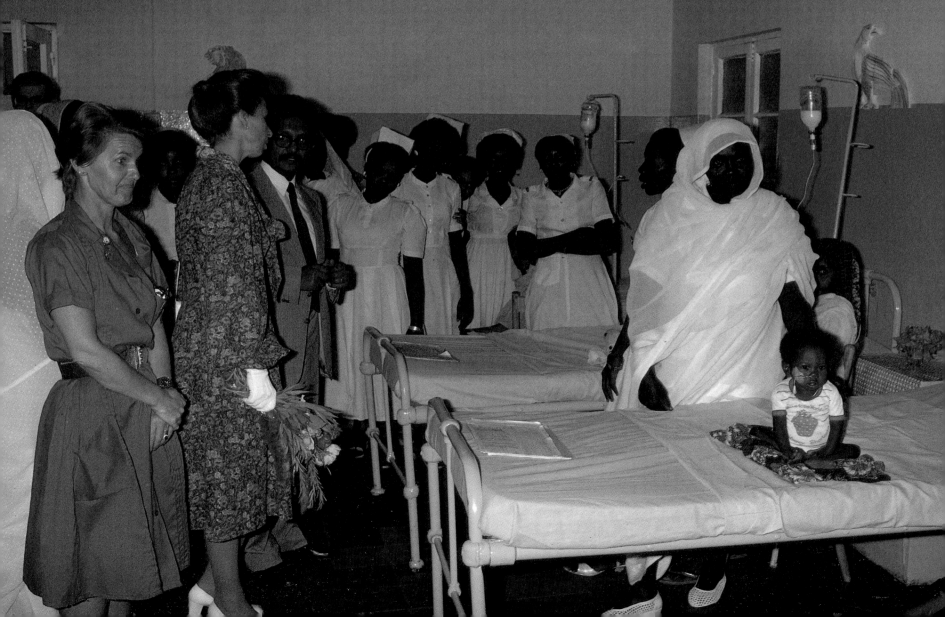

Princess Anne spent two days at Umbala, in Darfur Province, and in temperatures exceeding 90° F, for which (left) she was well prepared. The huge refugee camp here accommodated not only those Sudanese whom famine and war had uprooted from their tribal communities, but also some 20,000 starving people from neighbouring Chad who, ironically, found the conditions there, though bad enough by normal standards in Sudan, sufficiently promising by comparison with their own lot. Fortunately, by the time of the Princess' visit, the story had taken an upward turn. SCF had pumped seven million pounds into the Sudanese famine problem, and clinics, immunisation projects and feeding programmes were now coping with demand. So it was a relatively optimistic Anne who walked through the compounds (facing page, top), hand in hand with the children whom SCF had helped to save. The same was broadly true of Nyala, whose outlying villages were on the Princess' itinerary (facing page, bottom), and of Safawa, near the town of Gedaref, where she spent another part of her week in Sudan. The native and British workers she met (below) were able to report that, for the time being at least, disease and malnutrition had been brought under control, despite an unexpected influx of refugees, this time from Ethiopia, and an equally unexpected outbreak of cholera. And, when she arrived back in London, she in turn publicised her findings with the good news that real progress had averted a continuing crisis, but that, as always, more funds were needed immediately to maintain even the very basic standard of living now being enjoyed by the refugees.

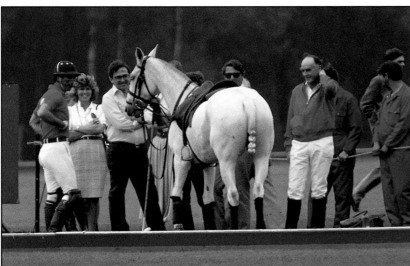

Prince Harry (right) leaves school on his first day back following a hernia operation – at three years old, his first experience of sustained medical treatment. As if proving what his father once said about having 'learned the way a monkey learns – by watching its parents', Harry's stride emulated Prince Charles' on the polo field that same week. Charles, who once said of polo that he hoped to go one playing it until the age of fifty, has been increasingly devoted to the game since his initiation at the hands of his own father in his mid-teens. Indeed, in one of his earliest tournaments, his side won a final against a side captained by Major Ronald Ferguson, who became his polo manager and is rarely far from his side on the numerous occasions when the Prince plays at Smith's Lawn (above). It is often said that Charles' enthusiasm for polo – 'I feel sheer terror, but I enjoy it tremendously,' he once said – is an irritant to his wife and family. But polo has attracted the Royal Family for over a century: George V played as a teenager as early as 1881; then his two elder sons and the Mountbattens. And so, one day, judging by his enthusiasm for treading in the divots (facing page, bottom), will Prince William.

Since Sarah Ferguson's marriage to Prince Andrew, polo has become even more of a family sport. Indeed, Andrew had seen his bride-to-be many times since childhood during visits to 'the polo'; Sarah's mother, now Mrs Susan Barrantes and seen (bottom left) meeting the Princess of Wales at Guards Polo Club, verified that the young couple had often met 'on the polo field – where everybody meets everyone.' Sarah herself, once a pavilion companion of Diana, now attends frequently in her own right (facing page, bottom left), while Diana can fill intervals between games with a field-side chat with

Major Ferguson (bottom right). Meanwhile, Prince Charles is at his most relaxed: treating one of his dogs (facing page, top left) to sugar lumps which he carries around in a glass jar (and which are generally reserved only for deserving polo ponies); enjoying a lager supplied by the afternoon's sponsors (facing page, top right); and performing a quick change of strip — he plays for more than one side on any afternoon. And the Queen's presence to hand over the trophies (below) evidences her continuing interest in the family sport.

Major Ferguson has been closely linked with the Royal Family ever since, in the early 1950s, he helped found Guards Polo Club. Prince Philip became an early member, and frequent companion of the major, and indeed was responsible for Prince Charles' introduction to both the sport and the club. After the Duke gave up polo, in 1971, (when, in his own words, 'my wrists went bad, my ponies went bad, and I was fifty all at the same time!'), Major Ferguson became Charles' polo manager, responsible for finding suitable ponies and slotting him into the tournament most appropriate to his improving handicap. The major is always on hand to give the Prince some last minute advice (bottom left), and to act as a buffer between him and the press, who frequently want to know how well the Prince is playing, or whether he fell or was pushed from his pony. And just occasionally (facing page) the two of them find themselves playing in the same team. Bottom right: the Queen, not a hair out of place, after presenting prizes at Smith's Lawn; while Diana (below) offers a more personal reward for Prince Charles' victory.

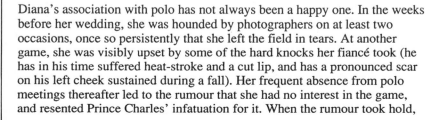

Diana's association with polo has not always been a happy one. In the weeks before her wedding, she was hounded by photographers on at least two occasions, once so persistently that she left the field in tears. At another game, she was visibly upset by some of the hard knocks her fiancé took (he has in his time suffered heat-stroke and a cut lip, and has a pronounced scar on his left cheek sustained during a fall). Her frequent absence from polo meetings thereafter led to the rumour that she had no interest in the game, and resented Prince Charles' infatuation for it. When the rumour took hold, she was back like a flash, swiftly denying her antipathy and refusing to let any degree of pregnancy prevent her from attending. These days, she brings the children as well, as she did (facing page) at the prestigious Cartier tournament in July 1987 at Smith's Lawn, which was attended also by the Queen (above left), Prince Philip (top right) and Queen Anne-Marie of Greece (top left). It seems she will be there for some years yet: Prince Charles promises to go on playing 'as long as I still bounce when I fall off'.

Being Queen of Australia as well as Queen of the United Kingdom accounts for the fact that Elizabeth II has toured there no fewer than fourteen times during her reign. The latest visit celebrated Australia's Bicentennial, and took her to most states and territories. At Perth, where the tour began, she opened the new (though unfinished) development Forest Place (facing page, top), then went on to Geraldton, which she proclaimed a city since its population had topped 20,000. At the goldmining centre of Kalgoorlie the emphasis was very much on the children who had come from several goldfield communities (right and facing page, bottom), while her subsequent visit to Brisbane for the opening of Queensland's World Expo (above and top) also included a walkabout after Sunday morning service at St John's Cathedral (top right).

Like most tours, this one had its own mixture of gravity and happiness. Solemnity marked an ANZAC Day memorial service and parade at Hobart, where the Duke of Edinburgh (facing page, bottom right) accompanied the Queen. More cheerfully, the Queen celebrated her 62nd birthday with a garden party in Perth (facing page, top right), and there were the customary walkabout scenes at Newcastle (top, and facing page, top left) and Melbourne (facing page, bottom left). At Geelong, a wool town where Prince Charles spent a couple of terms at school in 1966, a street walkabout (above and right) brought the Queen to a sheepshearing demonstration, at which she met a shepherd whose dog wore a wristwatch. Why? Because he rounds the sheep up clockwise, the Queen was told!

More than any other Australian visit, this had its share of protest and petty alarms. Smoke wafted from the Queen's plane on one occasion; her ferryboat was jolted on another; the Royal Yacht was daubed with graffiti; there were noisy IRA protests and even noisier and much more persistent clamour from the Aborigines and their supporters. But to the vast majority it was a colourful, friendly tour. The Queen and Duke seemed at their informal best at Albury (top and facing page, top); relationships between the Queen and Socialist Prime Minister Bob Hawke remained amicable (left and facing page, bottom right); the Queen was extremely pleased (facing page, bottom left) with Sydney's gift of a new State carriage and, despite her lack of inches, with the precision with which a lofty Guard of Honour greeted her (above) on her first full day in Perth.

Glamorous nights for the Princess of Wales: (top left) well-dressed royal star meets half-dressed screen stars at the premiere of *Superman 4;* (above) a glittering arrival for the 1987 musical *High Society* in London; (top right) attending the Royal Film Performance that year, and a chance to met Joan Collins and George Peppard, stars of *84, Charing Cross Road;* (right) an old favourite evening gown modified for a gala performance to mark Britain's presidency of the EEC in November 1986. Facing page: attending the premiere of *Otello*.

Princess Margaret's marriage to Antony Armstrong-Jones in 1960 was staged in typical 'fairy-tale' manner, and seemed a happy conclusion to the troubles that beset her during and since the Townsend years. The couple had two children – David, Viscount Linley, in 1961 and Lady Sarah three years later, yet before the decade was out, the marriage was reckoned to be in trouble. Lord Snowdon (he had been given the title shortly before the birth of his son) was rumoured to be seeking female company elsewhere; the Princess to be seeking alternative lifestyles in fashionable hippie communes. By the time the inevitable break came, in 1976, new friendships had formed on both sides: Snowdon's with Lucy Lindsay-Hogg, whom he later married, and Margaret's with Roddy Llewellyn, who accompanied her several times on her spring or autumn holidays to Mustique. The maelstrom of rumour, speculation, claim, counterclaim, denial and bitter, confused silences lasted well beyond the ultimate divorce proceedings in 1978, and only ended with the publication of a book by Christopher Warwick, said to have been accorded every assistance by the Princess and to have told, for once, her side of the story. Lord Snowdon has resolutely refused to comment on any aspect of his earlier marriage, and his personal and professional relationship with the Royal Family remains strong. David and Sarah are now adults, free agents, and leading their own independent lives. Occasionally, however,

they accompany their mother on her official journeys abroad, as happened in mid-1987 when she paid an official nine-day visit to China. Following very much in the footsteps of the Queen, whose State Visit there occurred the previous year, its high point (literally as well as metaphorically) was the walk along part of the Great Wall (facing page). At home, Princess Margaret undertakes engagements alone: (above) visiting the Children's Toy Fair at Earl's Court; (top right) on a day's visit to the Hampshire town of Basingstoke; (right) admiring some of the exhibits at the Chelsea Flower Show, where her guide is frequently the well-known gardening expert – and well-known friend – Roddy Llewellyn.

'I want to learn to fly, like Andrew,' said Fergie on her engagement day. So RAF Benson, home of the Queen's Flight, decided to give her a wedding present consisting of a £3,500 course of lessons. The new Duchess lost no time in taking the kind offer up. Three months after her return from honeymoon, she reported for her first day's instruction (right) in a course that was to last ten weeks. For the 'try anything once' Duchess, the course seemed a piece of cake, and her eagerness and boldness at the controls paid off by the end of January 1987 when, (bottom) accompanied by an admiring Prince Andrew, she went to the Air Training School near Oxford to collect her private pilot's licence. Thanks to her own sense of adventure – and to her instructor Colin Beckwith (below) – she now has her 'Windsor Wings.' Sarah's enthusiasm for the air did not stop there. Later that year, she visited Heathrow Airport and sat (facing page, top) at the controls of *Concorde*.

Unfortunately, training supervisor Captain Clive Elton was not authorised to let her fly the supersonic airliner, but she was allowed to operate the simulated controls of a Boeing 757 instead. And she was also invited to Jersey, to start the 33rd Jersey International Air Race, which she did with her customary gusto (right). The trouble was that the windy weather played havoc with her lightweight dress, and she had to borrow a raincoat (facing page, bottom left) from her lady-in-waiting Jocelyn Floyd in order to retain her modesty! Things were rather more elegant when she attended a ball that night (facing page, bottom right).

Left: showing all the makings of a king-to-be, Prince Charles arrives for the annual ceremonial armed forces display, the Royal Tournament. Its unique combination of evening entertainment and Service tradition explains why on this occasion the Prince wears his Service regalia with a black tie. The Tournament is a regular feature of the royal year; it is held each July over a period of up to a fortnight, and almost every performance is attended by a member of the Royal Family. It features mock military tactics and competitions, grand ceremonial and musical displays, and exhibitions of the work of the Forces' support services – surveillance, instruction and nursing.

But Prince Charles takes his leisure as seriously as his ceremonial duties. His dedication to polo apart, he is a sportsman of wide-ranging talents and interests, including the traditional aristocratic pursuits of 'huntin', shootin' and fishin'.' His fishing forays are usually confined to the River Dee these days, but hunting and shooting take him all over the country. He rides with several Hunts, the Cheshire, Cottesmore, Quorn, Berkeley and most notably the Beaufort – indeed it was at the hands of the late Duke of Beaufort that he acquired his hunting skills. Current controversy on the subject forces him to keep a low profile, and may well result in no more sightings of the Prince clearing hedges in his navy and red Windsor uniform (top right). At one stage, he diversified into steeplechasing and rode in five races (top left) in the eighteen months before his marriage. Unfortunately, the death of his favourite and most promising horse Allibar, a couple of races in which he was floored, and probably an understandable pressure from his wife in the early months of his marriage, led him to give the sport up. However, he has maintained his long-acquired and substantial skills as a shot, but prefers the 'real thing' – especially pheasant-shooting at Sandringham – to the clay-pigeon shoots, like this one (above) near Salisbury, in which he and other members of his family occasionally take part.

Previous pages: The Princess of Wales looks exquisite (left) as she meets the stars of *Dancers*, and a little doubtful (right) as she questions Dame Edna Everage about her choice of jewellery at a variety show in London. Both events are typical of the many which royalty attend in that they are put on for the benefit of various charities for whom the very presence of members of the Royal Family ensures a worthwhile box office take. One charity that always secures the Princess' support is The Prince's Trust. This was set up by Prince Charles a decade or so ago with the specific aim of helping disadvantaged young people – those unable to find employment, or frustrated in their efforts to create businesses through lack of funds – to set themselves up in creative enterprises. The Trust's target is to spread the funds sufficiently thinly to give hope to as many people as possible, rather than to accumulate large sums of money for just a few beneficiaries. Hence, individuals or small groups of business-minded young people have received £300 to help them buy material to make T-shirts, or £500 to hire equipment for a fish-and-chip shop, or £150 to rent loudspeakers or drum-kits to start a disco business, and so on. In this way more unemployed people get the chance to launch themselves, and this in turn gives them a more positive and

hopeful attitude to prospects which may otherwise have seemed full of despair and helplessness. One of the most frequently used methods of funding the Trust has been the rock concert. Rock groups such as Dire Straits, Genesis and the Boomtown Rats have given their services free in an effort to pull in large paying audiences – a goal invariably achieved if the Princess if going to be there too. An incorrigible rock fan, who by all accounts, likes to chassé down the corridors of Kensington Palace tuned into her personal stereo, the Princess would be a natural choice for guest of honour even if she were not Prince Charles' wife. The Prince is not so keen on the music, but the Trust is one of the causes for which he is prepared to indulge his wife's preferences. It's called teamwork!

Facing page: the Princess of Wales meets Alison Moyet (left) and Eric Clapton (centre right) at a Prince's Trust concert in 1987; (top) Phil Collins of Genesis presents her with tapes, and sweatshirts for her children; while Lionel Ritchie and his wife pile up the presents (bottom), including bomber jackets for William and Harry. This page: Charles returns the compliment and attends the Boomtown Rats concert at Wembley in 1985, for Live Aid, with its organiser Bob Geldof (top). Diana was also at the concert. Her other work for charity continues virtually on a daily basis. Above: sharing a joke at the end of a visit to the headquarters of Childline, and (right) being invited by Jimmy Savile, whose work for the severely injured at Stoke Mandeville Hospital she always acknowledges, to make an unexpected purchase!

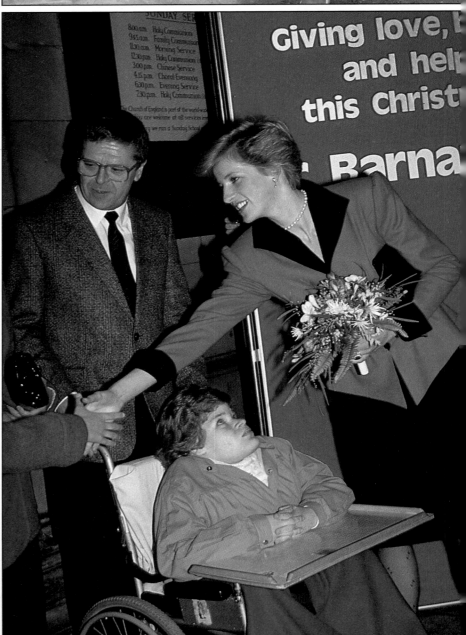

Facing page: The Princess of Wales has done a great deal to nail the myths and misunderstandings surrounding people confined to wheelchairs. The chairbound spectators to their wedding festivities in Buckingham Palace forecourt had some counterparts five years later, when a group of paraplegic athletes gathered (top left) to meet her and Prince Charles in connection with the 1986 Sport Aid event. During her visit to Ely more recently (top right), she delighted a disabled girl by stopping for a chat, while (bottom right) another wheelchair patient looks up at her as she meets families and charity officials at a carol service at St Martin-in-the-Fields. Bottom left: Diana on a visit to St Thomas' Hospital in London, clutching a huge welcome card that she had received with her bouquet.

Above: The Princess of Wales stoops to speak to a toddler who has just handed a bouquet to her. It's a typical gesture on Diana's part, though before she joined the Royal Family the sight of royalty bringing themselves physically to the level of their young admirers was all too rare. It seems to be the mark of the younger royals in particular that they discard the traditional royal aloofness in favour of more obvious displays of interest, concern or sympathy. This earnest conversation took place when Diana launched a Swimathon at the Queen Mother Sports Centre in aid of the Great Ormond Street Hospital for Sick Children, one of the world's most famous hospitals for children, and one with which Diana has been very closely connected since her marriage.

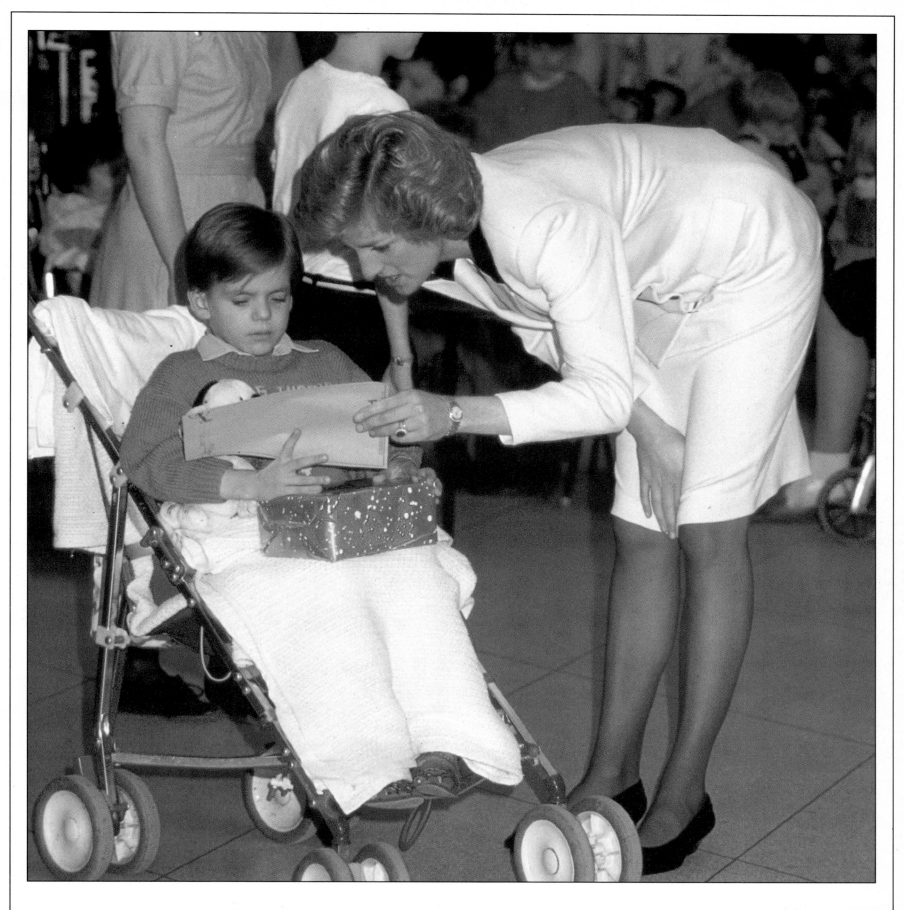

The Great Ormond Street Hospital for Sick Children claims the special affections of Prince Charles foremost among the Royal Family because it was there that he spent a week or so for an appendix operation at the age of twelve. He always remembers how well he was looked after, and has spearheaded much of the Hospital's attempts to raise funds recently, when shortages of equipment and space have become desperate. Diana puts aside time from a demanding schedule of duties to make sure she pays the Hospital a call at least once a year, though in 1987 she did twice as well! Her normal annual visit (facing page, top right) was supplemented by a special Christmas visit, to coincide with a visit from Santa (facing page, top left), and she spent most of her time there helping the children (above and facing page, bottom) to unwrap their presents. Right: the Princess sitting down to tea and a chat with the elderly at a day centre operated by Help the Aged, during the severely cold winter at the beginning of 1987.

The Princess Royal has always said that she wants to give her children as normal an upbringing as possible, and indeed they are very successfully kept out of the public limelight. But having a royal parent does bring its share of privileges. Not for many people, for instance, the opportunity to go yachting during Cowes Week, but when your grandfather holds all the most prestigious presidencies in the international yachting world, a day or two of excursions on the briny (facing page) are fairly easy to arrange. Likewise a ride aboard one of grandpa's carriages, pulled by the Queen's Oldenburg Greys, and driven by her faithful Crown Equerry of long standing at the Windsor Horse Trials, with a corgi asleep beneath your feet (below). Peter and Zara Phillips have been visitors to Royal Windsor for almost as long as they can remember (bottom left), so perhaps the occasional treat is a just reward. Being of royal blood may also mean you have to go to church on Easter Sunday in public (bottom right), but one guesses that's a small price to pay.

Canada, which Prince Andrew regards as his second home, played host to him and Sarah in July 1987, and will long remember the experience: an ebullient mixture of sightseeing, glittering banquets, instant rapport, and a great sense of light comedy. The Duchess looked the part on their arrival in Toronto, wearing Canada's national colours and a maple leaf in her hair (left), and repeated the gesture at a Government dinner that evening (above left). Next day, she attended a fashion show (top) with Prince Andrew and was herself commended for her own sense of style – 'simple, bright, arresting, direct,' said one designer. Even more direct was the concession she made to the cowboy concept (above) during a visit to a rodeo at Medicine Hat. Facing page: watching the Toronto Disabled Olympics on the second day of the tour.

A tourful of smiles. Facing page: the Duchess of York equally at home on a walkabout in Yellowknife (bottom right), among high society at Woodbine Racecourse (top right), at the Canadian Government's official banquet in Toronto (bottom left) and dressed up (top left) Klondike fashion for a carriage drive down Edmonton's 1885 Street at the annual Festival – and how period costume suits her!

This page: with the Duke of York, and still on honeymoon – or so they said. Top left: unisex costume for a visit to a goldmine at Yellowknife; the wet look on board the *Maid of the Mist* (top right), which took them within a few hundred yards of the Niagara Falls; and a stetson apiece for an afternoon's rugged entertainment at Medicine Hat's equivalent of the Calgary Stampede (above).

No royal visit to Canada is really complete without a taste of the great outdoors. The Yorks had already acquired the idea when they helped (left and below) to paddle their own canoes (authentic replicas, these, of those used during the old fur-trading days) into Thunder Bay, a former trading post on Lake Superior. For their efforts, they were given the paddles as souvenirs. The visit also taught them, graphically, why Thunder Bay is so named, for halfway through, the sky blackened, thunder boomed, and an enormous rain and hailstorm sent royals and locals scurrying for shelter. The real adventure began at the end of the official part of the tour, when the Duke and Duchess were kitted out (remaining pictures), ready for a week and a half of self-propelled adventure over 300 miles of the Thelon River in the Northwest Territories. In such terrain, it is said, the hardships of everyday life in the cities pale into insignificance. The Duchess' calf-length hiking boots, racoon-tail headgear, and protective hood against the king-sized blackflies that swarm in those quarters, suggested she was taking her part in the adventure seriously. The Duke looked rather more laid back: he had, after all, done this sort of thing several times before – and was 'almost famous' for it.

Much is made of the Royal Family's favourite colours. Perhaps the most famous preference is the Queen Mother's for blue. From time to time, every royal lady seems to go through a phase in which one colour becomes more popular than another, although exhaustive research will show that this is something of a myth. So, too, is the story that hosts always telephone a visiting royal's household to find out what colour she will be wearing, so that the bouquet matches the outfit. More often than not, the outfit will not be decided on until an hour or two before the visit. So, these pictures of Diana – (top left) in Gwent; (top right) at Walthamstow; (above left) at the Royal Ballet School; (above) at King's Cross and (facing page) at Hertford – while they show her looking stunning in red, do not necessarily mean that it's her favourite colour.

With few exceptions over the centuries, it seems to be common ground among members of the Royal Family that the initial impetus that Charles II and Queen Anne gave to the great Sport of Kings was a tolerably good thing. Certainly there are few occasions on which to see the royals at their well-dressed and animated best than at the annual flat-racing jamboree at Epsom – the Derby. A certain draw for the Queen and most of her near relations, the event looks set to enjoy royal patronage for many years to come. The latest recruits are those great royal friends the Princess of Wales and the Duchess of York who, on the strength of these pictures at least, could well be auditioning for the Di and Fergie Laughter Show.

No wonder the Queen (left) is not amused. On the other hand, her thoughtful, not to say somewhat dismayed, features could have something to do with the fact that of all her racing trophies, not one has ever come from a Derby win. Despite having anything from a dozen to a score of horses in training at any one time, and limitless resources for investment into breeding a Derby winner, Her Majesty remains deprived of the ultimate racing prize. A great leveller, the Derby!

The Queen's joyful gesticulation (facing page, top), so typical of an exciting Derby performance, is rarely captured at Ascot. The royal processions which precede each afternoon's racing at Ascot are elegant, the short journeys on foot into the Royal Enclosure subdued (left). Royal waves are obligatory (top); smiles, like Princess Michael's (above), optional. At least, that's how it was until the Princess of Wales acquired a new sister-in-law. Now it's all horse-play and horse-laughs (facing page, bottom).

Royal Ascot has as much to do with fashions as with favourites, and no member of the Royal Family worth her salt misses an opportunity to experiment with anything wearable, from hats to hemlines. Here, the Princess of Wales (above) shows just how far she has progressed since those early engagement days, with a fresh, jaunty, yet mature printed suit and cool, wide-brimmed, cream hat. With her in the Royal Enclosure is Caroline Beckwith-Smith, a cousin of her senior lady-in-waiting Anne Beckwith-Smith, and a close friend and former flat-mate of the Duchess of York, who is walking just behind them. All of which is not inappropriate, since it was at Ascot, back in 1985, that Prince Andrew and the then Sarah Ferguson got to know each other rather well, and began a relationship that led to their engagement the following March. Running parallel with Royal Ascot are four days of polo at Smith's Lawn, organised by Guards Club under Major Ferguson, and in which Prince Charles often competes. It's an occasion that Diana (facing page) rarely misses these days.

Just occasionally, Prince Charles goes abroad – mostly on business – without his wife. In 1987, for instance, he went to Swaziland, Malawi and Kenya. The Swaziland visit was hosted by the young king Mswati III – seen (above) at the Somhlolo Stadium. Ever the good sport, the Prince joined the king in a tribal dance and accepted a spear, shield and necklace from the Swazi Queen Mother, known to the locals as the She Elephant. On his first trip to Malawi, Prince Charles was welcomed by President Banda (left) and his colourfully dressed female supporters (top). Facing page: a Union Jack for the Prince at Blantyre, Malawi; a visit to Pisa's Leaning Tower during a private trip to Italy; and a contrast in headgear – a hard hat in the Texas oilfields in 1986, and a more decorative slouch hat in Australia two years later.

The Duchess of Kent, like most of us, enjoys her holidays, whether skiing or sunbathing, and her hobbies – notably her weekly rehearsals as a member of the Bach Choir. She also enjoys those engagements which enable her to look her best or to relax. But despite the elegance of a State occasion like the Guildhall banquet she and her husband hosted for the President of West Germany in 1986 (facing page) and the fun-of-the-fair atmosphere of the Berkeley Square Ball which she attended in 1986 (above), the Duchess of Kent is a dedicated worker for several charities. Foremost among them are the Samaritans, Age Concern and the Helen House Hospice for terminally ill children. When, many years ago, she was asked to become the Samaritans' Patron, she decided it would be no paper position. She underwent a three-month training course, which brought her face to face with the realities of suicidal tendency, with its causes (such as terminal illness, teenage pregnancy, family breakdown) and with the psychologists and doctors who

analyse and treat it. She regards herself as being in a good position to understand, since she herself suffered a series of personal tragedies, including a late miscarriage and the death of a much-loved father, which led to a nervous breakdown in 1982. 'I'm not very robust,' she recently said. It doesn't show these days. Twice in the past few years she has allowed the television cameras to show her at work for her special charities. Interviewed at Helen House, she told how, on the day of her departure for Australia, she visited a terminally ill child at seven in the morning – and was pleased to have done so, because the child died before her return. More recently, in connection with Age Concern, she was seen visiting the old during power cuts, and visiting homes for aged folk with no family to care for them. At one point an elderly lady broke down in tears, and the Duchess hugged her, pleading repeatedly, 'Don't cry; don't cry; don't cry.' It was a moving, as well as revealing, moment of total human involvement and shared distress.

Prince Edward did himself few favours when he opted out of the Royal Marines, amid public accusations that he had let the side down and proved himself a wimp. But there is no doubt now, and should have been none then, that the decision was good. Commendable though the idea of service is, it does not justify avoidable misery. The late Duke of Windsor was the most obvious example of someone trapped into a way of life that was not his. Prince Edward has found instead the Really Useful Theatre Company, and his theatrical career has every chance of flourishing: critics of the monarchy have, after all, complained often enough that it was represented by cultural philistines. Meanwhile, and despite his father's dismay at his leaving the Marines, he remains one of the family: showjumping (bottom left), the Boat Race (bottom), involvement with the Duke of Edinburgh's Award Scheme (left) and inspecting guards of honour (below) in Canada have distinct royal associations!

Diana's special effects: (below) a flamenco-style dress in red taffeta and black velvet by Murray Arbeid, with one black and one red glove to match, for the Americas Cup Ball at the Grosvenor House Hotel; (right) a slim, slit dress for a gala evening at Claridges to honour the Elizabeth Fitzroy Homes for the Mentally Handicapped; (bottom) a rich blue dress with a net and velvet bodice, for the Toscanini Memorial Concert at the Royal Albert Hall; and a classic white-and-gold strapless gown worn (bottom right) at the premiere of *Living Daylights* in aid of the Prince's Trust.

The value of Diana's evening wear wardrobe has often been a matter of speculation. Certainly the selection seems endless, and at a minimum of £500 apiece, the overall value could run into six figures. One of her richest gowns is the Elizabethan-style design worn (previous page) at the Birthright gala evening at Garrards, the Queen's jewellers; its sumptuous, yet sombre, effect set off beautifully by the amethyst and diamond cross, which Prince Charles commissioned from Garrards. Another is the Bruce Oldfield dress in crushed velvet, seen (facing page) at a British Fashion Week banquet in the

City of London: she also wore it for one of her official portraits by Donovan in 1987. This page: (top left) a graceful lemon-gold dress worn at Merchant Taylors Hall for a 1986 concert; (above left) a spangled, strapless dress worn at the premiere of *Cinderella* at the Royal Opera House a year later – both events in aid of the British Lung Foundation; (above right) a deep neckline dress at the Hilton Hotel's Starlight Cabaret in aid of Help the Aged, and (top right) a much plainer dual-fabric number for another visit to the Royal Opera House.

Although, even at leisure, the Royal Family are lucky to ensure privacy unless they are securely within the walls of their own residences, there are a few occasions when they seem really to let themselves go, without much thought for the photographers around them. It is, of course, the ultimate truism that they are at their informal best when surrounded by horses. For that reason, they seem to be truly themselves when spectators, mostly in an essentially private capacity, at the great equestrian events. Until quite recently, the Badminton Horse Trials was the most royally patronised festival of its kind. Following the successive deaths, since 1984, of the Queen's kinspeople, the tenth Duke and Duchess of Beaufort, founders of the Trials, the event seems to have been abandoned by the Queen and her family – possibly because they feel they now have little in common with the present Beaufort family, who would normally act as her hosts. This leaves the Windsor Horse Trials (usually in March or April) and the Royal Windsor Horse Show (May or early June) as the prime object of the Royal Family's attentions. They provide the opportunity for the royals to be seen at their most relaxed, and there are, after all, few other occasions when the Queen can be seen driving her own transport (above) or even helping others to take a short cut from one enclosure to another (facing page, bottom right), or when she and her family can roam fairly freely among the crowds to watch whatever part of the proceedings take their fancy (facing page, bottom left). The main item for them all is the three-day Carriage Driving Championship in which Prince Philip almost invariably takes part as a competitor. It covers all areas of the activity, from the more elegant areas of presentation and dressage, to the rough-and-ready speed and endurance trials which take the Duke up and down hills, round obstacles and through streams (left) while the Queen and various friends and family, including (facing page, top) Crown Equerry Sir John Miller and the Duke and Duchess of York, look on – and not without some anxiety.

Scenes from the 1988 Windsor Horse Show. This page: the Queen (right) with the Duchess of York, King Constantine of Greece and Princess Sophie of Hanover, Prince Philip's sister; (above) with Colonel Frank Weldon; and (top) on the final presentation day. Facing page: a family event as Prince Philip chats with Princess Anne (bottom centre) before the endurance round (top left) and after taking his team round the dressage course (centre left); the Duchess of York (top centre and bottom left) and her father (bottom right) put in an appearance; the Duke and Duchess of Gloucester look round the stalls (centre right) – the Duke sporting a recently-acquired stetson against the sun (top right); and Princess Margaret (centre) calls in for the final day's events.

These pictures, all taken within a year or so of the Duchess of York's wedding, show how quickly and obediently she has learned to dress to the royal norm. That is not to say she has lost her own sense of fashion direction: she has always refused to be put off by critics of the clothes she felt most comfortable in. It is rather that she realises that on some occasions the Sloane image – voluminous, colour-conflicting, heavy or shapeless clothes – is simply not what the public want to see. In making her choices for official outings, whether by day or in the evenings, it is transparently obvious that she has taken a strong lead from the Princess of Wales: one could imagine Diana wearing, or having worn, outfits very similar to these at one time or another, and Sarah knows that the trail her sister-in-law blazed has been both popular and successful.

Unlike the Duchess of York, the Queen is no stranger to criticisms of her fashion preferences. Indeed, she would probably deny that what she wears in public is what she would have chosen but for the basic requirement that she has to stand out in a crowd. The muted, sloe-coloured coat she wore for a recent visit to Hereford (facing page, top) shows how difficult it may be for the public to see her if she does not dress brightly, while her choice for an Easter Day service at Windsor (facing page, bottom) illustrates the error of selecting a colour too close to the royal ecclesiastical maroon! Beyond that, the Queen tries to wear clothes that somehow suit the occasion: at Portsmouth (below) she wore a predictable blue to match the naval theme; at the Derby (bottom left) she usually chooses a sound, rich colour; and when she visited Covent Garden to open the Jubilee Market and see new developments near the Piazza, she wore this vivid ensemble (bottom right) which may have reminded those who saw it that they were not too far away from the Chinese quarter of London.

Keeping up appearances is part of the job specification of royalty, and most of them acquit themselves of this quite creditably. It is, admittedly, more difficult when you're not feeling up to it, or when, as happened in the run-up to the Prince and Princess of Wales' week-long visit to Germany in 1987, public speculation about the state of your marriage becomes positively obsessive. When, the weekend before this tour, the couple failed to appear together for a family wedding, they ensured a public feeling of certainty that the split was becoming visible.

In a way – though doubtless they would argue that it had never been so intended – the general fixation about Charles and Diana's supposed marital problems guaranteed heightened interest in the tour. Major royal visits to West Germany have been comparatively rare, the Queen herself having paid only two calls in her entire reign of almost forty years, so this first joint visit by her eldest son and her daughter-in-law would in any event have been popularly received. But the big marriage problem brought it, and them, under close, unrelenting scrutiny.

They rose to the occasion throughout. Diana positively glowed on their arrival in Berlin (above left) and was her usual elegant self that night at the Opera House (above right and centre left) to see a performance by the Royal Ballet. Bonn saw the royal couple happily together next day (top), while the day after found Diana more subdued (facing page, top left) at Cologne Cathedral than later (facing page, top right), at the British Embassy Preparatory School. Facing page, bottom: Diana at the Bavarian Opera, and Charles at the Tornado aircraft assembly plant near Munich.

These two photographs showed Diana at her most stunning, and did more than any royal denial could to convince any who still had doubts that she was as happy and fulfilled as ever. The daring, yet impeccably smart, off-the-shoulder black dress she wore at an official banquet in Bonn (facing page), coupled with half-a-million pounds worth of jewels given to her the previous year by the Sultan of Oman, and the Spencer tiara set upon her newly styled hair, confirmed her claim to fashion maturity. The following evening, she chose black again (above) for a less formal, but in many ways equally important, occasion – a fashion show, held at the Cologne Museum of Art – which featured the best of British design know-how and creativity. Diana was, of course, right to choose something basically simple and to appear relatively unadorned. An overdressed guest, however royal, at a fashion show tends to become a competitor rather than an observer. Perhaps she knows that there is not very much even the best fashion houses can teach her about how to dress.

The Prince and Princess of Wales spent two days in Munich, the capital of the state of Bavaria, whose former royal house would, as Prince Charles said, probably have enjoyed a stronger claim to the British throne, had it not been for the Act of Settlement of 1701, by which the Crown passed, on Queen Anne's death thirteen years later, to the House of Hanover. By now, Diana's dazzling evening appearances were such as to prompt television stations to break into their evening programmes to bring German viewers live coverage of the royal engagements. The Prince and Princess' visit to the Bavarian State Opera House (below) to see *The Marriage of Figaro*, and their attendance at the official State banquet in Munich (facing page, and bottom pictures), were two such occasions.

Diana's fashion surprises continued for her visit with Charles to the Opera on their first evening in Munich, with this controversial dress in royal blue taffeta and mauve velvet. Charles' paisley pocket handkerchief provided an unexpected, though much less controversial, touch of colour, but controversy of another kind was about to blow up around him as a result of some appreciative remarks he made about the NATO alliance depending in part upon the efficiency of the German soldier – a quality for which they were, he said, justly recognised. Unfortunately, even half a century on, bitterness over Germany's part in World War II lingers in Britain, and Prince Charles was accused of insensitivity towards those in Britain whom the war had left wounded for life or bereaved. As on many occasions in the last few years, he found himself torn between his preferred line in making meaningful rather than bland speeches, and the need to avoid causing offence.

The royal visitors' last full day was spent in Hamburg, a vibrant, scenic city with a reputation for the slightly anarchic avant-garde. It certainly proved to be anarchic: no sooner had a barge bearing the Prince and Princess across the River Elbe reached a suitably isolated spot than a group of protesters, squatting on the roof of a tenement building, began chanting IRA slogans condemning the British presence in Northern Ireland, and launching flares at the royal craft. Though it was the only example of hostility in the whole tour, the protest, with all its security implications, caused immense concern. The Hamburg police had, after all, guaranteed the safety of the Prince and Princess and, as more than one observer pointed out, the flares could just as easily have been lethal missiles, and the consequences much more serious.

All of which might well have put a blight on the day's activities – but didn't. The royal couple were here primarily to promote the British Week that one of the city's departmental stores was staging – a show which no Royal is ever slow to support in person. They also visited the continent of Europe's oldest Anglican Church, founded in 1611 by English merchants. And that evening's reception and official banquet at the Town Hall (these pages) provided not only another occasion for Diana to outshine all others, but also an opportunity for both her and Prince Charles to make it clear that the events of the morning had been put behind them. And, of course, that, contrary to the reports which had preceded this spectacular and successful visit, they were very much the united couple they had always been.

Some say that a three-day eventer cannot adapt to the requirements of steeplechasing, but the Princess Royal, never one to be put off by generalisations, has proved otherwise. For two years, she has raced regularly (if not frequently) at some of the best courses in the country, including (below and bottom right) Hereford, Redcar and even Sandown. Although, sadly, her promising loaned horse Cnoc Na Cuille collapsed and died recently, the Princess has already won a couple of races, and seems set to make a new career out of this demanding sport. Bottom left: the Princess with her two children at Aintree in 1988, where she unveiled a statue of the famous National winner Red Rum. Facing page: the Princess of Wales (top left), forced to hide her fashions under a sturdy raincoat; Prince Charles following the Queen Mother's passion for salmon-fishing (top right) on the River Dee at Balmoral, and (bottom) the Queen, Prince Philip, Queen Mother, Princess Diana, Prince William and Zara Phillips leave the Chapel Royal after Easter Sunday morning service at Windsor.

Sarah learns the art of making the most of things. In Cardiff (top left) she enquires of a toddler how this tulip flowerhead came to be parted from its stalk. Left: quiet pleasure at receiving a small posy during a visit to Scotland. Above: lending an ear to the crowd's good wishes at Clarence House, during the celebrations for the Queen Mother's 86th birthday and (top) astride Aldaniti, during a mile-long ride from Windsor Castle, by way of the Long Walk: this formed part of a 250-mile journey by the former Grand National winner, partnered by various riders, from Buckingham Palace to Aintree in aid of the Bob Champion Cancer Trust. The Duchess enjoyed a champagne breakfast at a Windsor hotel after her jaunt. Facing page: Sarah wearing a blazer-style jacket during a visit to Cedar School at Romsey.

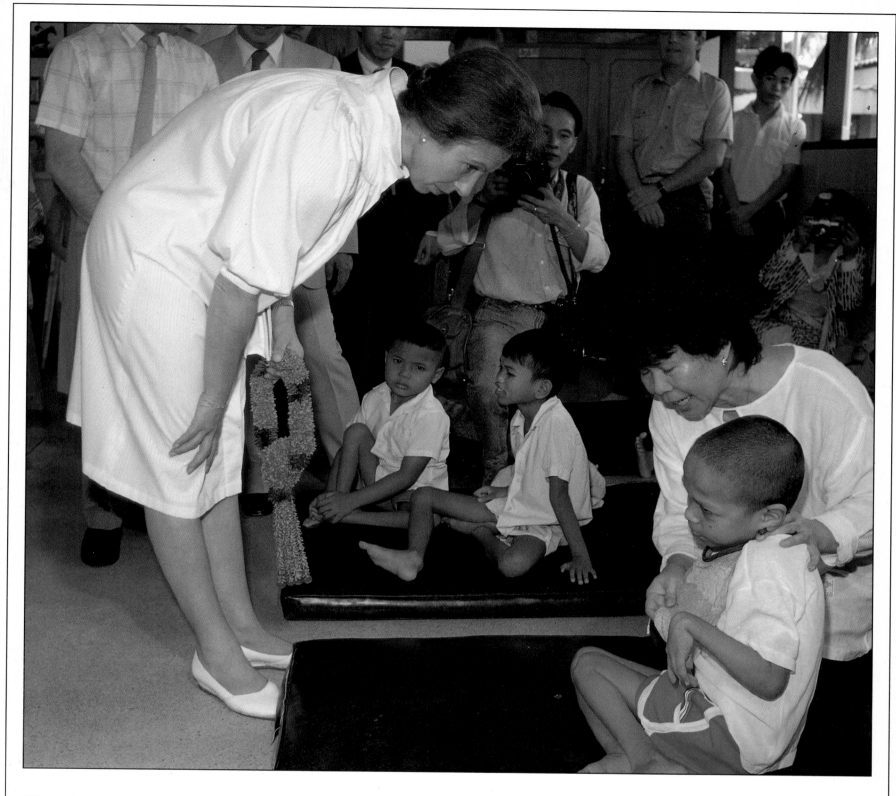

Towards the end of 1987, Princess Anne undertook a ten-day tour of the Far East on behalf of the Save the Children Fund. Her first stop was in Thailand, for a visit arranged by Princess Chulabhorn, one of the King's daughters, who was at Bangkok's airport to meet her British counterpart. Apart from a brief audience with the Thai monarch, however, the Princess Royal spent her time with those at the other end of the social scale. A quarter of the city's seven million souls live in slums, and the swamp slums – conglomerations of houses on stilts – are the worst of them all. In Asoke suburb lies Rim Tang, more commonly known as the Railway Slum, since it lies by the main line into Bangkok. Funds from the Thai Government are hard to come by except, as you might expect, when a princess comes to visit. Magically, on this occasion, trucks had been in the slum for two weeks, carrying out piles of sludge and filth, and brand new boardwalks had been laid for Princess Anne to tread. Nothing like it had happened before.

Along the boardwalk (left) came the Princess carrying a garland and passing between scores of well-presented children waving flags. At the end of it, right in the centre of the slum, is the kindergarten which SCF established and spends £8,000 a year to maintain, with free meals and education for the children of 5,000 squatters. Almost pathetically, these impoverished youngsters offered little gifts of towels (facing page) to the Princess as tokens of welcome. Above and overleaf: Princess Anne at the Pakred Home for Handicapped Children, near Bangkok, where children abandoned by their parents because of disease or affliction, or rescued from beggar-gangs, are housed and cared for by SCF.

Thailand is a landlocked democracy surrounded by war-scarred Communist countries whose past history has resulted in a massive influx of refugees into the relatively peaceful and prosperous kingdom. As a stop-over between her visit to Bangkok and her journey to Vientiane, the Princess Royal called in at one of the many refugee camps on the Laos-Thai border. Ban Napho Camp, in Thailand's Nakhom Phanom province, houses a whole generation in indefinite transit, and SCF operates alongside former community services to supplement basic health, nutritional and educational facilities. You couldn't help absorbing the impression that the camp had been tidied up for the visit (facing page, top), but in any event, the need for order and regulation is a daily essential. The hospital complex, which the Princess visited (top) is necessarily quiet – rather uncannily so, she thought, as she studied the weak, listless mites who had only recently arrived there. 'Are they usually as quiet as this?' she asked, with an obvious look of resigned concern. She also saw the dental clinic, where traditional, more basic methods of tooth extraction prevail if modern, painless treatment is not available. And she heard several refugees' stories of escape to this precarious haven. It was all a world away from the normal royal round of Western-world walkabout small-talk.
Above: Princess Anne at her next stop, Laos; and (right) in Burma later in the tour (see overleaf).

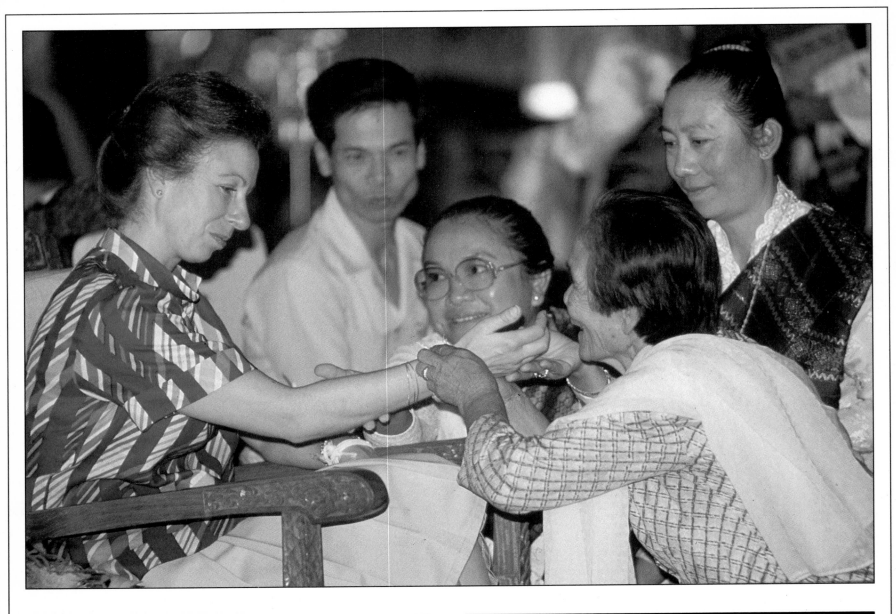

The Princess Royal was the first member of the British Royal Family to visit the Marxist-Communist state of Laos, which overthrew its own ancient monarchy in 1975. Welcomings were low-key, the clearance of cattle from the runway area of Vientiane airport and the provision of flags for children being among the few concessions to the royal visitor. Here again, the Princess confined her activities to visiting schools and hospitals funded and kept in existence by SCF. There was, however, a pleasant interlude in the form of a visit to the Ban Siampon Temple, where Buddhist monks combine worship with the sort of social work reflecting that of Save the Children. On arrival here, she had each of her wrists tied with cotton charms (top) that were supposed to bring her good luck and was provided with coconut milk to drink. She visited the temple's creche, and was introduced to Noi (previous pages), a monk whose pride and joy was a collection of bullet-ridden vehicles left after the long Indo-China wars of the 1950s and 1960s. In Burma, the tour's last days were more relaxed, with a breathtaking visit to Rangoon's Shwedagon Pagoda (previous page, bottom), and an official dinner (above and right) given by the Communist government.

The pagoda that Princess Anne visited is probably Burma's most famous, and boasts a roof studded with five thousand diamonds and containing more gold than the vaults of the Bank of England. The banquet, held in her honour by the strongly Marxist President Ne Win, was probably more a reflection of the fact that, as a freedom fighter, he trained alongside the British against the Japanese in the last war, than of any real sympathies with the capitalist system represented by his royal guest. But it achieved some breaking of ice, as is evident in the warm smile on Princess Anne's face at the pre-banquet reception (top right). It was not so long ago the case that the Queen blazed the royal world trail, stepping into territories that no member of her family had entered before. Now that role seems to be Princess Anne's who, as President of SCF, is a regular globetrotter with commissions to venture into areas hitherto virtually closed to Western travellers. The job is not particularly pleasant by royal standards. There are inconveniences in traversing deserts, entering ghettoes, experiencing the legacies of horror, and being obliged to see the results of neglect and disease that many of us would not care to undergo even for a royal pension. But she, who has more than once confessed to being unmaternal, takes a motherly, yet unpatronising, level-headed and, above all, commendably close personal interest in this sadly-neglected area of human existence.

Above: Princess Anne's arrival in New South Wales: Easter 1988.

It's good to know that the Prince and Princess of Wales take their titles seriously enough to ensure that the principality receives frequent visits from them. Prince Charles has, since his Investiture – an event which brought him sharply into contact with the realities of life at all levels there – shown a real concern for the prosperity of Wales, and has been behind many of the commercial ventures that businessmen from other parts of Britain and around the world have brought to an otherwise often-neglected part of the United Kingdom. Several Japanese firms which have established industrial plants in South Wales, for instance, would probably not have done so but for a royal word in the right ears during Prince Charles' bachelor-day visits to Japan in connection with British export drives. The three-day visit which the Prince and Princess first paid together to the principality in 1981 have been followed up by regular visits. These pictures were taken during Diana's visit to Gwent in 1987, a year which saw a dozen or so days on which the royal couple journeyed to Wales. The trend continues: between December 1987 and July 1988, for instance, they undertook almost twenty engagements, from a tour of a tyre factory at Aberdare to a visit to a fitness festival in Clwyd; and from an inspection of a new police HQ at Carmarthen to a tour of a Laura Ashley factory in Powys, and a visit to an agricultural show at Builth. Charles, in whose name many community schemes operate, often spends whole days at a time visiting projects, as he did in June 1988 on a whistle-stop tour of Dyfed, West Glamorgan and mid Wales.

Royal visits to Hollywood are few and far between, but invariably matters of great spectacle and pizzazz. The Yorks became the latest royals to sample the legendary extravagance of Los Angeles when, just a week after Prince Andrew's 28th birthday, they flew in (top left) for one of the busiest and most informal trips they have yet undertaken. Barring the occasional customary formality, like the signing of visitors' books (above right), the week-long event was one of wisecracks and asides, antics and laughs – a 'try anything once' mentality. An umbrella dance by children from Los Angeles' Chinese quarter, for instance, resulted in a downpour which called for real umbrellas (top right), while Sarah's visit to the neo-natal unit at the University College of Los Angeles (above left) provided one of several opportunities to discuss prospective motherhood. Contrasts in dress ranged from the rich Yves St Laurent evening gown she wore (facing page, top right) at the UK/LA Festival dinner to raise funds for the rebuilding of the Globe Theatre in London, to the simple outfit which graced the Yorks' final day in California (facing page, top left). Nor was the Duchess slow to make her hosts feel appreciated. What could not be said was written or illustrated on hats and hairstyles. On her first full day in Los Angeles, she wore appropriately-lettered hatpins (facing page, bottom right), while a visit to the County Museum of Art to see a David Hockney exhibition allowed Sarah to fly the flag for Britain and America with these diamante hairpins (right).

Facing page: six hours of the Duke and Duchess of York's Los Angeles visit were in fact spent out at sea – several miles out in the Pacific on board the USS *Nimitz*. The largest warship in the world today, with no less than four acres of quarterdeck and two of its very own TV stations, the *Nimitz* provided Prince Andrew at least with the opportunity to compare life in the American navy with that in the Royal Navy, in whose uniform he was dressed for the occasion. At his request, he was catapulted from the ship's flight deck in an aircraft at 160 miles an hour and at a force three times that of gravity, while the Duchess, then four months pregnant, looked on (bottom right).

Perhaps the most fascinating day of the Yorks' visit was spent in the world of high-tech effects. The robot that greeted them in Culver City (bottom left) presented the Duchess with her posy, introduced her to her guide and, when her back was turned, called out 'Nice hat!' Then the Duke rode a simulated roller coaster which swung and jerked its passengers (below right) as they watched a synchronised high-speed journey on a screen ahead. For the last day of the tour, the El Dorado Polo Club put on a charity match against a team captained by Sarah's father (below left) at Palm Springs. The Major's team lost 8-7, so in true sporting spirit, Sarah presented the trophy (bottom right) to the victorious Americans.

The informal nature of tours such as this, and the chance conversations the royals have with those they meet, can sometimes offer quite an insight into the royal lifestyle. On this visit, for instance, we learned from the Duke and Duchess that life was not as spartan at Windsor as one might imagine: though they have some pretty old-fashioned loos of a mechanical, rather than flushing, type which nevertheless work extremely well. Dungeons, no longer required for their original purpose, have now been converted into a disco. The Duchess has no pets ('apart from *him*,' she said, pointing to her husband) except for a labrador. Her favourite board game is Scrabble (or so she told David Hockney). They had not yet decided where to educate their first child, but thought they might be persuaded that Los Angeles University is the answer. Sarah can have too much of a good thing in the food line: 'I'd love a cheeseburger!' she was reported to have sighed after yet another elegant lunch. And cream cakes and the Duchess do not see eye to eye. Meanwhile, the Duke tried his hand at icing cakes; the Duchess, interrupted in her speech by someone shouting 'I love you!', called back, 'I'll see you later'; they both met the likes of Jack Nicholson and John Travolta; Sarah went shopping, in between engagements, in Rodeo Drive, Los Angeles' answer to Bond Street; and she was quick enough to point out that, contrary to what was written inside a book presented to her, there is no 't' in Duchess.

Diana wore this large-check coat (facing page) for her arrival in Switzerland for her skiing holiday in 1987. Note the casual combination of clothes beneath, a sure sign that this is a private outing and not a public engagement. Clothes for official duties are much less informal, even though the wrap-coat (above) in which she arrived in Oporto during her visit with Prince Charles to Portugal that year seems less fitted than a similar style she wore during a visit to Bournemouth a year later (right). Note the popular, casual, polo-neck blouse in each case. Top left: an even warmer coat with a high collar for an outdoor meeting with the Mayor of Canterbury, contrasting with (top right) a more summery coat over a calf-length dress for her visit to inspect a new body-scanner at Stoke Mandeville Hospital in Buckinghamshire.

The cost of maintaining the Royal Family has often been a sore point in the past, when claims for increases were made as and when they were thought necessary. Since the mid-1970s, however, an increase has been awarded annually and broadly in line with inflation. New figures are announced simultaneously with the Government's Budget proposals – a device which no doubt helps keep the issue in the background. These increases are often wrongly referred to as pay rises. They do not, in fact, represent money to reward royals for their services, but to pay the expenses of providing them. Serving members of the Royal Family travel to and from engagements: chauffeurs and cars have to be paid for. They must wear a suitable selection

of clothes: these have to be bought for the purpose. They have to run offices to administer their work: secretaries and equipment have to be funded. Nowhere is this clearer than in the case of the Queen (facing page), whose allowance of £4.5 million is accounted for largely (about 75%) by staff salaries. For the rest, the Queen Mother's £390,300 relates to the cost of keeping her in a style appropriate to the widow of a sovereign, while Prince Philip's £217,000 reflects the staffing and equipment for one of the heaviest and most varied of royal schedules. Most other senior royal households are awarded amounts similar to Princess Anne's (left) of £135,600, while the junior branches – the Gloucesters, Kents and Princess Alexandra (above) – are in effect funded from the Queen's private finances.

Though the Queen has always preferred that family summer holidays should be taken at Balmoral, Prince Charles has begun to break the mould. In 1986, his cousins the King and Queen of Spain invited him and his own growing family to spend a few weeks at the Spanish royal summer retreat, the Marivent Palace – a hillside villa near Palma de Majorca. The essentially private holiday was preceded by a photocall at the villa, when these pictures were taken showing the Wales' family with the Spanish King Juan Carlos and Queen Sofia and their only son and heir, Prince Felipe. Queen Sofia was entranced by the Wales' children: 'delightful and lovable,' she called them, 'and William is so friendly and full of fun.' Both children made a big fuss of Juan Carlos' Alsation Arky, and Prince Harry actually rode him for a short time.

Queen Sofia has made the point that the 1986 holiday was good for William and Harry in particular because neither of them had experienced a seaside holiday before. 'They have been relaxing and enjoying our weather,' she said. 'The children have never been on the beach before, and it has been special fun for them.' It obviously must have been, because in August of the next year they were back again. This time the photocall, on the day of the guests' arrival in baking temperatures, was enlivened by an unscripted fight between Arky the Alsation and Queen Sofia's lapdog, Perros. Harry went to Perros' rescue, throwing gravel over Arky as Juan Carlos tried to separate the two dogs.

The Spanish summer holiday could easily become an annual event for Charles, Diana and their children, just as Princess Margaret used to take an Italian break every summer. There is a lot in common between the Spanish royal family and the Wales' household. King Juan Carlos and his family enjoy skiing every bit as much as Charles and Diana; the king is also a keen sailor (and indeed a former Olympic yachtsman), while Prince Charles still enjoys windsurfing, and his preoccupation for personal fitness will have found great support with Diana.

The close blood relationship between the Spanish and British royals – the King, our own Queen, and Prince Philip are all counted among the numerous great-great-grandchildren of Queen Victoria, while Queen Sofia, along with Elizabeth II and the Duke of Edinburgh, is descended directly from Christian IX of Denmark – is clearly a strong influence on the inter-family friendship, but at the same time, King Juan Carlos' commitment to a constitutional monarchy acting within a democratic governmental framework has found great favour in Britain, and in the years to come is almost bound to help overcome the last, prickly problem of conflicting Spanish and British claims to Gibraltar.

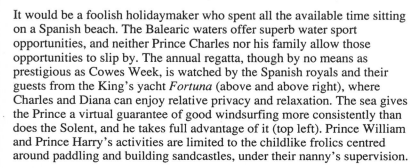

It would be a foolish holidaymaker who spent all the available time sitting on a Spanish beach. The Balearic waters offer superb water sport opportunities, and neither Prince Charles nor his family allow those opportunities to slip by. The annual regatta, though by no means as prestigious as Cowes Week, is watched by the Spanish royals and their guests from the King's yacht *Fortuna* (above and above right), where Charles and Diana can enjoy relative privacy and relaxation. The sea gives the Prince a virtual guarantee of good windsurfing more consistently than does the Solent, and he takes full advantage of it (top left). Prince William and Prince Harry's activities are limited to the childlike frolics centred around paddling and building sandcastles, under their nanny's supervision.

'The children look very well,' said Juan Carlos, at the start of the 1987 holiday. 'They love the water and the sun, and I am glad they were able to come back.' It was all rather different from the little expedition they were taken on a few days earlier, while still in London. Their nanny, and a bodyguard, drove them to Coram Fields, a summer playgroup in Camden Town, where they played on swings and roundabouts with other children. Majorca was something else again!

Facing page: Diana at Kew Gardens to open a new conservatory, just before her 1987 Spanish holiday, wearing the same outfit as she wore on her semi-official visit to Spain with Charles the previous April.

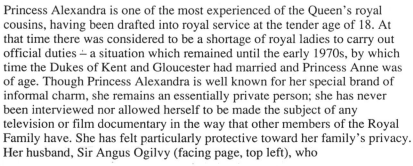

Princess Alexandra is one of the most experienced of the Queen's royal cousins, having been drafted into royal service at the tender age of 18. At that time there was considered to be a shortage of royal ladies to carry out official duties – a situation which remained until the early 1970s, by which time the Dukes of Kent and Gloucester had married and Princess Anne was of age. Though Princess Alexandra is well known for her special brand of informal charm, she remains an essentially private person; she has never been interviewed nor allowed herself to be made the subject of any television or film documentary in the way that other members of the Royal Family have. She has felt particularly protective toward her family's privacy. Her husband, Sir Angus Ogilvy (facing page, top left), who

accompanies her only on certain evening engagements but not otherwise, has business commitments in the City; her recently-married son James has spent his schooling and university career quietly in the background; and her daughter Marina (facing page, bottom left) has been able to join groups of young people, as she did for Operation Raleigh, without the fuss and special treatment being a member of the Queen's family might entail. The Princess, whose father was killed during the war and whose mother died at the early age of 61 in 1968, is keen to maintain family ties with her elder brother, the Duke of Kent, and his wife, and her younger brother, Prince Michael (facing page, top right), whose marriage to Marie-Christine in Vienna in 1978 Alexandra attended.

The trouble with being labelled, as Diana often is, with descriptions reminiscent of film stars is that the world expects you to compete with them. Diana has frequently been in a position where, the epitome of one type of excellence, she has come face to face very publicly with people (Joan Collins and Elizabeth Taylor are the two most obvious examples) regarded as equally glamorous in their own field. So when, in 1987, she visited the

Cannes Film Festival, all eyes were on her sense of chic in this most quintessentially chic milieu. Most would agree that she made the grade. Her crisp daytime outfit by Catherine Walker, with its navy-striped puffball dress, was smartness itself, while her blue chiffon evening dress with matching scarf and sparse but richly-hued jewellery made her, as one observer put it, 'the star of the Cote d'Azur'.

The village of Scampton lies a third of the way between Lincoln and the Lincolnshire coast, an unpretentious village which could be forgiven for boasting its famous RAF base. For it was from here that the Dam Busters left for their legendary raid on the Mohne Dam in Germany during the last war. And in true gung-ho fashion, the Duchess of York came here with

Prince Andrew, only a few months after she qualified as a pilot, for a day with the Red Arrows. First came the easy part of the proceedings. The Duchess, feet firmly on the ground, had her photograph taken with the Red Arrows' team (facing page, bottom) and then watched them putting their formation aircraft (facing page, top) through some of the most stomach-turning routines you ever saw at close quarters, the more suicidal of which even made the Duchess duck and squirm.

Then came the hard bit. After a very uneasy lunch in the officers' mess, she boarded a Bulldog training aircraft. Her olive green all-in-one and black boots (top left) were hardly in the best traditions of royal fashion, but it was the gear for the job, and the Duchess is nothing if not professional. With Squadron Leader Dave Walby at the controls (top right), she was taken up for a tour of the aerodrome (above), then over the northeast of the county and towards the South Humberside coast. Here, the controls were handed over and, in what was probably the most exciting half-hour of her life, she was taught to loop the loop, perform sudden, steep climbs, and cope with swoops, wing-overs and stalls. And when she returned, flushed with success, she did so as the first aerobatic female member of the Royal Family.

The seventeen 'serving' members of the Royal Family cover between them thousands of miles a year criss-crossing the country. Now and again, inevitably, their paths cross – as happened when Princess Anne met briefly with her father on a helicopter pad near Cambridge (below left). Father and daughter share the same keenly direct temperament and many interests; one of these, yachting, has in recent years claimed a great deal of the Princess' leisure time: (bottom left) sailing with a yachting acquaintance, Kate Rogers, in the Solent during 1987 Cowes Week, and (facing page, bottom right) at a boating exhibition in Weymouth. The theme also recurs as part of her official duties, on her visit, for instance, to Gosport in 1987 (bottom right) in the uniform of the Women's Royal Naval Service, and (below right) at the 1988 Daily Express Boat Show in London. Facing page: Princess Anne, in her robes (top right) as Chancellor of London University (a post she contested with two other candidates) visits St Bartholomew's Hospital; and (top left) leaving Sandringham Church with daughter Zara after Sunday morning service. Bottom left: both children enjoy a sheltered view of the Windsor Horse Show.

Above: Diana at a banquet given by the Portuguese Government at the Bolsa Palace in Oporto, in honour of the visit she and Prince Charles made to Portugal in February 1987. Normally, the Royal Family are quite adept at timing their foreign tours to catch the best of the weather, but for Charles and Diana in Portugal it went wrong. The entire four-day visit was bedevilled by wind, rain and icy temperatures from the very beginning when Charles piloted the Queen's Flight aircraft into the country. Nevertheless, it was a friendly and interesting visit, as you might expect when the representatives of two long-term international allies meet. Indeed, one of the reasons for the visit was the commemoration of the Treaty of Windsor, which, 600 years previously, concluded the settlement for the marriage of John of Gaunt's daughter to King John I of Portugal. Prince Charles' historical ears naturally pricked up at this, but he was all the more fascinated to learn, during a tour of the Cintra Palace in Lisbon, of a thousand-year-old family link between the present-day Windsors and one of the very earliest Portuguese kings. Diana had her moments of interest too, particularly with a visit to her former make-up expert Barbara Daly, who had established a branch of her Body Shop business in Oporto.

Princess Margaret once caused a furore when she refused to wear sterile garments to cover her hair and clothes during a visit to a medical research laboratory. For Princess Diana, this has never been a problem. Although, on one occasion in Australia, she burst into fits of giggles when Prince Charles put on a protective helmet that was too small for him – 'Does your wife always make fun of you like this?' he asked an onlooker – Diana knows that health, safety and hygiene are areas in which the royal example is as good as any. Thus, on a visit to an industrial plant in Hartlepool (top left), she wore a hard hat, though it did nothing for her hairstyle; and when she opened a new dairy complex at Shepherds Bush, she was taken around in a crisp white smock and a jaunty hat to match (above right). No prizes for guessing that she enjoyed the new headgear (above left) when she was admitted as a Fellow of the Society of Gynaecologists – it all seemed very becoming, unlike the not-so-random breath test she was given during a visit to police headquarters in Kentish Town (top right).

Facing page: the unmistakable, glittering personal panoply of the State occasion, with the Queen richly attired in sequinned gown crossed by the shot-silk and starred Order of a foreign state, and fairly laden with priceless jewellery. The Queen hosts two or three State visitors, whether fellow crowned heads or elected presidents, annually, and is herself the guest of a similar number of foreign heads of state in return. As host, the Queen entertains at Buckingham Palace, the invariable royal base until the late 1960s, or Windsor Castle, with its pastoral attractions to make up for London's cosmopolitan character. In the days before travel developed to its present state of convenience, it was the custom for the monarch to entertain, and to be entertained by, any one country's representative once only during the reign. In George V's time, this was not a difficult achievement, since he rarely travelled overseas: 'Abroad is horrible!' he is supposed to have declaimed once: 'I know; I've been there.' Elizabeth II, by contrast, far and away the most travelled monarch, is now well into her second round of State visits in Europe, and has since the early 1970s been receiving visitors from abroad for the second time. One cannot help thinking that she would emphatically disagree with her uncle, Edward VIII's deploring remark: 'What rot, and a waste of time and money these visits are!'
However spectacular any State visit is, it cannot compare in ultimate wealth of symbolism and pageantry with the ceremonial glories of the State Opening of Parliament. Constitutionally, the Queen is not only Head of State, but the apex and residual seat of parliamentary power – which is why no Act of Parliament can be put into effect unless and until it has received the Royal Assent. Unlike Queen Victoria, whose antipathy towards London increased with the years, Queen Elizabeth II insists on reinforcing the statement of the Crown's ultimate authority by opening every session of Parliament in person. She even interrupted a tour of Australia in 1974 to travel back to London and perform the Opening, after a General Election took place which had not been foreseen when the tour began. For the ceremony, the Queen has almost invariably travelled, with the Duke of Edinburgh or other members of her family, in the Irish State Coach (below), so named because it was manufactured in Dublin, in the days when the whole island of Ireland was part of the United Kingdom. This particular custom may well change if the Queen decides that the coach presented to her by the Government of Australia during her bicentennial visit there in May 1988 should be used for this purpose in the future. The tiara she wears on the journey is exchanged at the Palace of Westminster for the Imperial State Crown, which will have preceded her in the procession, and which normally will be worn only this once in any year – an illustration of the supreme significance of this most fundamental of all the ceremonies in which the Queen is ever involved.

If it is true that the Duchess of York has taken her line in daytime dress from the Princess of Wales, it is equally certain that she has been creating her own precedents in the realms of evening wear. The flame-coloured wrap which she wore to such awe-inspiring effect during her visit to Hollywood, and which she wore again back in London (above and facing page, top right) at the premiere of *White Mischief*, may have been snidely referred to as 'an Yves St Laurent duvet' but it proclaimed everything about Sarah's wide-open exploration of the fashion possibilities available to her. No combination of colours, and no way of wearing them, has escaped her attention. Stark black and white may not suggest themselves as obvious for a redhead, but the effect was stunning enough when she attended a dinner at the Museum of Army Flying (facing page, top left), and positively elegant

with the decorous line of flower-frills worn at a banquet in Mauritius in September 1987 (facing page, bottom right). Much of her panache she owes to her restless habit of decorating herself with matching accessories. Quite apart from the succession of changes which her hair stylist, Denise MacAdam, has wrought with her hair – it can successfully be worn in attractive long ringlets and coils, in a plait, piled up, in a chignon, as a wild mane, or gathered by bows – Sarah loves to plant matching pieces, whether flowers, feathers, leaves or jewelled clasps, in her coiffure (facing page, bottom pictures) to give emphasis to the dresses she wears. The result? Lots of eye-catching schemes that convince us all that Fergie just loves being royal!

Like Diana, Sarah did not own very much jewellery when she became engaged. And, like Diana, she is beginning to acquire it and make full use of it. A highly valued possession is a delicate necklace of diamond flower clusters which the Queen gave as a wedding present, reported to be worth over £50,000. She wore it (previous pages) with the orange stole, at a Mansion House reception (top left), at a London theatre (top right), and at a performance of *Kiss Me Kate* at Stratford (above left). Andrew's gift of a simple pearl necklace with lozenge-shaped diamond pendant was worn on her wedding day, and with the black and pink dress (previous page, bottom left). Sarah also owns this attractive ruby and diamond necklace (facing page), believed to have been a wedding gift from an Arab state. Sometimes (above) she settles for a simple choker.

Viscount Linley and his sister Lady Sarah Armstrong-Jones would probably be termed 'yuppies' if they were not so closely connected with the Royal Family. Their snappy, rather Sloanish, appearance for the christening party given for Prince Philippos of Greece (facing page) underlines their lively, London lifestyle. But they have to shape their own lives, which is why Lord Linley has spent the last ten years or so graduating towards the career in furniture making that has marked him out as a talented young man. His parents have encouraged him all the way, and he now runs a furniture workshop with his partner Matthew Rice (below), which both Lord Snowdon and (right) Princess Margaret come to visit from time to time. His latest enterprise is an unashamedly up-market Chelsea restaurant, called Deals, established in partnership with his cousin Lord Lichfield. Bottom right: Viscount Linley with his girlfriend Susannah Constantine. The two have been close companions for many years, but wedding bells seem as remote as for sister Sarah, whose career seems set to begin at the Royal Academy of Art.

The year of Diana's marriage was also the Year of the Disabled: indeed a group of disabled people were brought into the palace forecourt to see the bridal carriage return after the wedding. She still maintains the link: (left) at Fairfield School for Handicapped Children, Northampton and (bottom) at a junior games event for the disabled at Taunton. Questions of balance for Diana at a London performance (below) of the Moscow Circus, and (bottom left) at the premiere of *Wall Street*. Facing page: Diana at her first solo Cup Final – Wimbledon (in blue) v. Liverpool.

'I didn't think that anyone would find us interesting after we were married,' said Princess Michael. She discovered otherwise to her cost but, despite a succession of pressures, the marriage itself has not suffered. There is no doubt that the Michaels enjoy the high life in the company of a wealthy circle of influential friends. Many of their public engagements are society sprees, such as the Berkeley Square Ball which they attended (facing page, top) in 1984, but their private pursuits take them on even more enviable excursions and dream holidays abroad. Both the Prince and Princess enjoy sailing, and have supported various British attempts to break world records and win the Americas Cup. In 1986, Princess Michael (facing page, bottom left) was strongly identified with the (eventually unsuccessful) attempt by Richard Branson (top left) to put Challenger II into the finals of the Americas Cup, while both her and her husband's support for Peter de Savary's earlier attempt at the Cup were rewarded with an invitation to spend a winter holiday on the Caribbean island of Antigua, where de Savary had just opened a private club (above). The couple (top right), who were welcomed to the island by a full ceremonial brass band, spent an idyllic week swimming, windsurfing, touring the island on horseback and (facing page, bottom right) just soaking up the sun.

Hands full: Diana clutches her bouquet and an oversized programme (facing page) at the premiere of *Otello*. Hands clasped: learning how a James Bond film is made (top left), at Pinewood Studios. Hands apart: Diana receives a certificate from Liza Wellcoat (left) during a visit to the Red Cross. Handshake: arriving for a reception at Grocers Hall (above), where one of the earliest commissioned portraits of Diana can be seen. No hands: the perfect royal smile from Diana (top) during a recent reception at the Victoria and Albert Museum.

The Princess Royal once said that she was delighted that she never had a sister. She must, on the other hand, be thrilled with her daughter, who is making great progress in the Princess' favourite sporting activity. Young Zara shows every sign of following her mother into the equestrian arena. She not only attends horse trials and shows with her parents; she keeps herself fully occupied inspecting courses (top left at Gatcombe), sizing up fences (top right at Windsor), tacking up ponies (left at Windsor), or riding around any spare piece of ground available (above at Smith's Lawn). She's learning to pose for photographers as well (facing page, top left at Tidworth), and can even manage a melting ice-cream with one hand, and her pony with the other (facing page, top right at Tetbury). And when she's doing none of these things, there's always a recalcitrant corgi around (facing page, bottom), needing the sort of firm discipline for which Princess Anne has become well known!

Royal pregnancies, once regarded as a matter for concealment, are these days more open affairs. Though the change in attitude was forged by Princesses Anne and Michael, much stimulus came from the Princess of Wales, whose engagements continued to within five weeks of her first confinement. Not to be outdone, the Duchess of York travelled all over the country until mid-1988, sporting her multitude of maternity clothes, many of them, it must be said, makeshift and less elegant than Diana's. Left: a floral dress for a visit to Hereford. Facing page, top left: a plain cerise outfit (she ordered others in yellow and navy) worn at Berkhamstead. Facing page, top right: evening maternity wear at the Barbican in London. Remaining pictures: a kiss, a rosette, a wave and a private moment at a horse show in York – Sarah and Andrew's last public engagement together before they became parents.

The York baby arrived in a riot of eights – on the eighth day of the eighth month of the eighty-eighth year of the century – and at 8.18 pm. As if to celebrate this extraordinary coincidence, her proud parents, seen (above) leaving London's Portland Hospital four days later, gave her the eight-letter name of Beatrice. Queen Victoria, whose youngest daughter was called Beatrice, would have been gratified, but the widespread speculation in favour of Elizabeth, with its recent York connections, was dashed; there

would be no new Princess Elizabeth of York. Instead, the Queen and the Queen Mother are remembered in the new princess's second name, while her third and final name commemorates Queen Mary, who, for the eight years between 1893 and 1901 was, like Sarah, also Duchess of York. And so Princess Beatrice Elizabeth Mary of York was taken away from London for the first of a lifetime's visits to Scotland, as her delighted parents presented her to the family at Balmoral.

Princess Beatrice was just over four months old when the time-honoured ritual of a royal christening (this page) took place in a pre-Christmas ceremony at Buckingham Palace. She was dressed in the elaborate robe of Honiton lace first used for the baptism of Queen Victoria's first child almost a century and a half before, and in which the children and grandchildren of every British sovereign have been christened since.

The new royal baby was, equally traditionally, celebrated in poetry, the Poet Laureate having composed a lengthy tribute based on the number eight, which figured so prominently in the date and time of her birth. But, unlike in former times, the godparents were not overwhelmingly royal: the proud parents' choice included an architect and one of Sarah's former flatmates.

Sandringham is where, for the Royal Family, one year ends and another begins. Time was when, shortly before Christmas, the whole of the Sovereign's family moved *en masse* from Buckingham Palace to spend six or eight relaxing weeks in this Norfolk country retreat, so beloved of all monarchs – 'Dear old Sandringham,' wrote King George V; 'the place I love better than anywhere else in the world' – since Queen Victoria bought it for her eldest son a century and a quarter ago. Then, in the last twenty years, the present Queen decided that the family was too big to fit into Sandringham's accommodation, and that the Christmas festivities would be held at Windsor. These would last three or four days, and then the Snowdons, Gloucesters, Kents and Ogilvys would go their separate ways for the New Year. Sandringham would thus be reserved for the Queen, Prince Philip and their immediate family – children and grandchildren only. Since 1988, pending major restoration work at Windsor Castle, Sandringham is again the royal Christmas, as well as New Year, venue. Their days there, especially in early January, before the grandchildren have to go back to school, are pleasant enough by most people's standards, and offer as leisurely a break as Balmoral does during the summer, but are nevertheless probably not quite as blissful as they were a century past. Our curiosity about the way Royals spend their private lives is too great to afford them the uninterrupted leisure they seek. A brief, weekly glimpse of them on their way to or from Morning Service at one of the local churches (facing page: the Queen with her eldest grandchild, Peter Phillips, leaving church after Mattins) is as much as we are normally entitled to, but, by unwritten tradition in recent years, a cat-and-mouse game has developed between the press and the Royals in which the prize has been the best or most intimate photograph of one or other member of the Family at rest or at leisure. A shot of the Queen riding out with the Duchess of York, or of Prince Edward taking time off from his theatrical activities to join the Duke of Edinburgh, Prince Andrew and Mark Phillips in a spot of pheasant-shooting, or one or other of the young princes and their cousins indulging in a spot of horse-play in the snow is the stuff of which newspaper and magazine sales are made, and photographers who feel they have a crust to earn are usually hard-nosed enough to indulge in some pretty brazen intrusions upon the royal holiday.

Their victims' pleas, demands and veiled threats – 'I wish you a very Happy New Year and your editors a particularly nasty one,' said Prince Charles to prying photographers once – have consistently failed to achieve a lasting, or even temporarily satisfactory result. One of the latest devices, a photocall in which, in a royal effort to buy the press off during the remainder of the holiday, the newsmongers were invited to photograph and report on the royal youngsters clambering over a fire engine belonging to the Old Fire Station on the Sandringham estate, and which the Queen's father bought and restored to its former glory, while the Queen, Duke of Edinburgh and Prince of Wales looked on (this page), was hardly more successful than those of previous years – which is probably why the royal trio are looking less than easy, and perhaps even a touch sceptical. The New Year holiday continues until mid-February, embracing the sad anniversary of King George VI's death in 1952: it was at Sandringham that he died, and the Queen Mother ensures that she invariably spends that day in what is for her a house of powerful memories. That apart, there is always work to be done as preparations for another long and busy year are finalised and provisional decisions for the year beyond that are made. Grand ceremonies, spectacular tours, national celebrations, and a host of provincial engagements lie ahead for Britain's ultimate family. And all that, in addition to the personal triumphs and problems that never fail to become public issues, and which have at last, perhaps, convinced us that these roving and highly respected ambassadors for Britain are by and large as human as the rest of us after all.

WHERE AND WHEN TO SEE THE ROYALS

Most of us only see members of the Royal Family at second hand – by way of television or newspaper, for instance. But if you know where to be, and can get there, it is not difficult to see them for yourself. For everyone's information, the monthly royal magazines *Majesty* and *Royalty* list most royal engagements for the forthcoming four weeks. For more specific daily details, if you are in London, buy a copy of *The Times* and open it at its Court and Social page, where you will see a list of all the day's engagements complete with time and place. Be there at least an hour beforehand – at least two if the Queen or Princess of Wales are involved – and secure your position outside the building at which they are due to arrive. Obviously, the further forward you are, the better and, as you will in any case have only a brief opportunity to glimpse (particularly if officials get in the way at the last minute), concede no ground. If a royal is visiting your part of the provinces, your local newspaper will have been running almost minute-by-minute details well beforehand. A royal walkabout, if there is one, will provide you with by far your best opportunity, so find out where it will happen, choose your spot and take up your place as early as possible. And if you want the best chance of being royally spoken to, wear, wave or offer something that will catch the royal eye and give your distinguished visitor something to talk to you about.

With the exception of major royal holidays in the summer, the chance to see one or other member of the Family is almost a daily one. But here are some special occasions offering good opportunities if you can plan ahead:

JANUARY With the Queen and her immediate family at Sandringham throughout most of the month, Sunday morning services offer favourable opportunities. The venue may change from week to week: the royals usually worship at the church on the Sandringham estate, otherwise at Sandringham Parish Church, or at local villages such as Wolferton, West Newton and Castle Rising.

FEBRUARY A good month for spectacular evening galas in London's West End; these continue into March and, to a lesser extent, to later in the spring.

MARCH The first of the year's State Visits usually occurs now (sometimes April, depending how Easter falls). If the visit is to London, a position somewhere along the processional route from Victoria Station to Buckingham Palace (usually the long way round, via Whitehall and the Mall) is rarely difficult to obtain. If the visit is to Windsor, the Long Walk up to the Castle provides an excellent spectator opportunity. The eventing season gets into full swing, so watch out for horse trials all over the country – the Phillips family is always likely to turn up in force. And the Cheltenham Festival in mid-month means that the Queen Mother will almost certainly visit the racecourse on one or two days, especially for the Gold Cup: she often leaves the Royal Box for the various paddocks and enclosures, and a path through the crowds is cleared for her.

APRIL The Thursday before Easter entails the Queen's attendance (normally with Prince Philip) at the Royal Maundy Service, held at a different provincial cathedral each year. A good, colourful occasion, usually combined with a half-day tour of the city in question, and a walkabout. Large numbers of the Royal Family attend Mattins on Easter Sunday at the Chapel Royal at Windsor – a worthwhile chance to see the children as the family arrive and leave. The Badminton Horse Trials are held in April (sometimes early May) at Badminton House, a few miles east of Chipping Sodbury in Gloucestershire. Royal representation has been sparse in recent years, but if Captain Mark Phillips is competing, you're almost sure to see the Princess Royal and her children, as well as Prince and Princess Michael and theirs.

MAY Most royals attend the Windsor Horse Trials early in the month, and nearly all are to be seen at the Royal Windsor Horse Show, where Prince Philip competes in the carriage-driving tournament, at the end of May (or early June). The Chelsea Flower Show is held in the third week, but you have to be an insider to get a really long, close look at anything up to a dozen royals who come here on Preview Day. The polo season begins in May (even late April), so look out for Les Diables Bleus or Maple Leafs or any other team that Prince Charles may be playing in, either at Guards Polo Club at Smith's Lawn, Windsor, at Cowdray Park, Ham (near Richmond, Surrey), or at Romsey. Odds are high that Diana, and possibly William and Harry, will be there – Sarah, too, if at Guards.

JUNE Trooping the Colour takes place at Horse Guards in London at 11 am on the second Saturday (with full-dress rehearsals on each of the two preceding Saturdays; Prince Philip or Prince Charles deputising for the Queen at the latter). Tickets for a seat on the parade ground have to be applied for (at least four months in advance) from the Brigade Major at Horseguards. Otherwise, watch the processions *en route*. The route from Buckingham Palace down the Mall into Horse Guards is usually thickly lined, especially around the Queen Victoria Memorial, from which the Royal Family can be seen on the balcony afterwards at about 1 pm. The Garter service and ceremony,

usually held annually at Windsor Castle, takes place two days after the Trooping. The public is not admitted to the service in St George's Chapel, but luck and an early application to the Lord Chamberlain's Office at St James's Palace may provide you with a free ticket to watch the processions in the Castle grounds. Royal Ascot follows on the next four days. If you can't get into the Royal Enclosure, or even into the public one, assemble at the Golden Gate, near the public entrance to the racecourse, where the Royal Family alight from their cars and get into their carriages. A rewarding opportunity: plenty of royals, and plenty of time to see them. Guards Polo Club runs a tournament at nearby Smith's Lawn during Ascot Week, and many of the younger members of the Family divide their afternoons between the racing and polo.

JULY The Queen and Prince Philip traditionally spend the first week of July in Scotland, carrying out numerous engagements in and around Edinburgh, with a garden party at the Palace of Holyroodhouse and often a service of the Order of the Thistle at St Giles' Cathedral. Local press will give details. Other members of the Royal Family will hover around London, spending occasional days in informal surroundings at the Centre Court during the final week of Wimbledon, usually very early July (exceptionally late June): the Kents, who are Presidents, are the most frequent visitors. Almost every day of the two weeks of the Royal Tournament at Earls Court during mid July is graced by a royal presence. There may be another State Visit this month (alternatively in June).

AUGUST The 4th is the Queen Mother's birthday, and the Family comes to celebrate it with her. The 'front' gate of Clarence House is the place to be (early), or Sandringham if it's a weekend. The Queen Mother will come out to collect flowers and gifts from well-wishers, and various members of her family will help her 'unload' them. Good fun and a happy atmosphere. Cowes Week straddles that day, starting at the very end of July: the Duke of Edinburgh, the Michaels of Kent, Princess Alexandra and Prince Edward are regulars at this international Isle of Wight yachting festival The Princess Royal and her family, and some foreign royalty (especially Greek and Norwegian) may also be seen trying their hand in the Solent. Binoculars essential. Later that month, the royals often sail to Scotland for their holiday, and call in at the Queen Mother's Castle of Mey on the way. Be at Scrabster to watch them all disembark for an affectionate family reunion.

SEPTEMBER A good family representation at the Braemar Games during the first (sometimes the second) weekend of the month is traditional. As most of the royals are thereafter on holiday at Balmoral, there is little chance of sighting them, unless you happen to be in Ballater or another nearby town while some of them are doing a little unexpected shopping. Sunday morning service is almost invariably held at Crathie church, where you can see two or three carfuls of royals come and go.

OCTOBER A month of fairly routine engagements in London and around the country: like February, colourful evening engagements in theatreland offer the most attractive opportunities. The Royal Variety Performance, attended by the Queen and Prince Philip, or alternatively by the Queen Mother, and two or three other royals, is staged at the London Palladium at the end of the month (or very early November).

NOVEMBER A busy ceremonial month, usually beginning with the State Opening of Parliament (if this has not already taken place at the end of October) which, being the major constitutional event of the year, involves a full procession from Buckingham Palace, via Horse Guards and Whitehall, to the Palace of Westminster. Basically, the Palace is closed to the public for the occasion, as is Parliament Square, but there is a mile or more of processional route to compensate. Most adult royals, including the King of Norway (a grandson of King Edward VII) attend the Festival of Remembrance at the Royal Albert Hall on the Saturday before Remembrance Day, but you need to be inside the Hall to see them. Most are seen again at 11 am the following day for the Service of Remembrance at the Cenotaph in Whitehall: the Queen, Prince Philip, Prince Charles, Prince Andrew, the Duke of Kent and Prince Michael all take part in the ceremony, while the Family look on from two balconies above. An invariably well-attended occasion, so an early arrival is recommended. The last State Visit of the year normally takes place in November.

DECEMBER A 'short' month, with most routine public engagements ending around the 20th. About the 22nd, the various families move to Sandringham for Christmas. The little church on the Estate is the venue for Christmas Day Morning Service and the public are allowed within a useful distance (though not into the church itself) to see the procession of cars arrive to set them down. Some members return by car: others, especially the younger families, may walk back to the House if the weather is clement, providing a good chance to see them and their children.